# Watercolours

## *from scratch*

# Watercolours
## *from scratch*
### Art Workshop with Paul

## Paul Taggart

Sandcastle
Books

First Published in Great Britain in 2006 by
**Sandcastle Books Limited**
The Stables
Sheriffs Lench Court
Sheriffs Lench
Nr. Evesham
Worcs. WR11 4SN

www.sandcastlebooks.co.uk

ISBN 0-9552478-0-2

Printed and bound in Thailand

# Contents

# Watercolour
## PRINCIPLES

**Watercolour is a fresh and exciting medium**, whose beauty is reliant on its natural transparency. Watercolour paints offer limitless possibilities when all of the attributes and characteristics of this hugely popular medium are fully exploited. Not surprising, when you consider that most people start with simple pencil sketches, which are then overlaid with colour washes.

*The principles of watercolour painting can take you on a journey from the simplest of Line and Wash coloured sketches through to the rich, lustrous results of a technique that combines those of Wet on Dry and Wet on Wet. This versatility makes it attractive not only to the complete beginner, but also to the professional.*

*Watercolour painting is unlike any other medium, in that it affords the painter a brilliance and transparency of colour. Contrary to popular belief, painters are not restricted to producing delicate paintings. The technique of Wet on Wet, for example, allows for a stronger concentration of pigment, which dries to a clean, rich finish.*

*The potential to achieve fine detail for delicate work, right through to the bold strokes with which to produce dramatic compositions, means that watercolour painting can be applied to any subject - from the most delicate study, to a formal portrait.*

The simplicity of a boat and its reflection is a subject of universal appeal and makes an ideal project to exploit the strokes made by various brushes - pages 74 to 77.

A textural subject used to best explore the surface of a paper and to exploit its texture in the project on pages 90 to 93.

*The principles of Watercolours from Scratch will take you step-by-step on your journey into watercolours, with the simplest of painting kits to accompany you. First, you will be taken through the basics of each of the tools in your kit, then you will be introduced to the world of colour, before moving on to a series of projects.*

*There are many steps, which will require your time and patience. Be prepared to follow the steps at a leisurely pace and you will reach your destination, one that will bring much pleasure and a sense of self-fulfilment.*

*Within the body of this book, I have imparted all the information you will need to begin successfully. There are exercises to help you become familiar with the basic painting kit and others with which to practice a variety of techniques. It is important to think of these as exercises, they do not need to be perfect. No-one has ever learned to paint without making mistakes, time and again.*

**Always complete an exercise or painting,** even if it goes wrong. More is learnt from correcting mistakes than by constantly starting again.

**Throughout the book brushes are shown** painted as though full of opaque colour. This is in order to visually identify the colour loaded, how much is present and where it is held in the brush. With transparent colour, the paint would be only gently visible to the naked eye.

*Once the exercises have been mastered, move on to the stage-by-stage projects. These are meant to be both a challenge and an inspiration to your progress and are based directly on what you will have learned by completing the preceding exercise.*

*Success with these will be a real mark of achievement, but again, do not be put off if they go wrong the first time. Without those problems you will be none the wiser, if you are not prepared to breach any potential barriers.*

*Everyone is full of enthusiasm when taking up a paintbrush for the first time, but lack of confidence often gets in the way and at the first frustrating experience many give up. The combination of these two feelings contrives to heighten the sense of inadequacy and it is my intention in this book to get over that hurdle.*

*Watercolours From Scratch is meant as a sound introduction to watercolour painting for beginners and those returning to painting. It should also prove a useful refresher to those who already paint and help clarify a new approach.*

Varying yellows, oranges and reds in this lustrous still-life prove ideal to exploit palette mixing in the project on pages 82 to 85.

# Which paints do I need?

*A very good question to pose when starting out. Many painters are not able to get the proper advice early on and consequently find themselves with inappropriate paints.*

*Paint is like any other piece of equipment, it is made to fulfil a specific function. Try to make it do something it simply was not designed for and you are heading for trouble. This could lead to frustration, or worse still, you could give up on the idea of painting completely.*

**A PLETHORA OF DIFFERENT PAINTS** are offered as watercolour paints and indeed they are, for they mix with water. However, not all are traditional watercolour paints, for the pigments from which a number are made are often weak and unstable. They are difficult to dissolve and colour mixes produced from them tend to be dull and granular. Traditional watercolour paints contain more pigment and thus their colours have more depth and resonance.

Three main ranges of quality water-based paints are available for artists. There are acrylic paints, which could serve as watercolour paints and can be used with watercolour techniques. However, once dry, acrylic paints cannot be re-dissolved and further techniques are required to work with these paints effectively.

Gouache paints, also referred to as Designers' Colour or body colour, are meant to be used more thickly and produce a wonderful matt finish when dry. They are by nature opaque and the transparent washes sought after in watercolour painting are unfortunately not achievable. Because gouache paints feature the same base medium as traditional watercolours they can always be used in conjunction with them.

Finally, the traditional watercolour paints, which can be used for the simplest sketch to the more serious painting. These offer a richness of colour quite different from any other medium. The secret of true watercolour paints lies in their transparency.

It always seems strange to those discovering watercolours for the first time, that white is not required in this medium. For those who like to have white in their palette of watercolour paints, Titanium white gouache has long been a favourite. As fashions have changed, Titanium white is now also available in traditional watercolour form. Chinese white is also available, but is semi-opaque.

While the exercises and projects
contained in this book appear to have white
in the paintings, it is the use of the inherent
whiteness of the watercolour paper that is exploited.
To add white to a watercolour paint mix or colour
introduces an opaque or semi-opaque element, which
adds opacity to them. Generally, as an opaque paint,
watercolour loses its lustre and richness.

### SELECTING YOUR PAINTS

Should you select watercolours in tubes or in pans?
There is no doubt that using pans is great fun, for you
can carry a box of colours anywhere and at anytime.
Flip open the lid and there are the paints and a brush,
for instant use.

If interested in experiencing the Wet on Wet
technique, you will notice the benefits of using colours
squeezed from the tube. You will certainly become
hooked on tube colour the first time you experience its
soft misty qualities.

The fact is, you will eventually want to build up a
collection of both tube and pan paints. By carrying out
the exercises and projects that follow, you will be in a
position to determine the strengths of each, to make an
informed decision as to which you will need

# Understanding paints

## Basic constituents

Watercolour paints are made from pigment (colour) held together with a binding agent, the gum (medium).

Quality paints contain lots of pigment [left]. Cheaper paints are bulked up [right].

Quality paints mix cleanly and brightly [top]. Cheaper paints are less successful [bottom].

## Basic types

Quality paints are available in fluid form in tubes, or dry form in pans and half-pans.

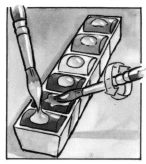

Tube paints create large washes quickly. Suitable for swift coverage of large areas.

HINT : PAN PAINTS - Add drop of water to top of pan to soften slightly and aid loading of brush. Ideal for small mixes in brush head.

*The most versatile type of paint* is that found in tubes. The quantity of paint held in the tube is easily accessible and more fluid and as such can be swiftly dissolved to produce large quantities of thin washes. This is desirable when working with a paint that dries quickly. However, it is also invaluable when working wet-on-wet, as the colours can then be used almost at tube consistency. Using the paint stiffly is quite a different experience from what you would usually expect from watercolour painting.

The manner in which tube paints are prepared for use can make all the difference in getting the most out of them. The paint should be squeezed out generously into the deep well of a palette.

Create a mound of it in the centre of the well and surround this with a moat of water to keep the paint fluid, which is important, as soft paint will keep

cleaner. Should a dirty brush be introduced to this soft mound of paint, the paint itself will not become tainted. A brush deposits colour only when it touches a hard surface, therefore should the mound become dry, residual colour from the dirty brush will be deposited on the surface and the mound of paint becomes contaminated. Keep the water in the moat replenished.

> **TIP**:
> Always dip your brush into the centre of the mound of paint. Never touch the water in the moat, as this will also be taken up and thin the colour being loaded onto the brush.

## Basic qualities

*ARTSTRIPS©*

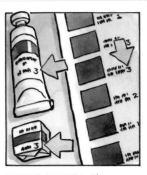

While Artists' Quality paints are made from the finest pigment [top], Students' Quality paints are made from cheaper varieties or dyes [bottom].

ARTISTS' QUALITY - Pigments vary tremendously in cost. The tube, wrapping or colour chart will show the most and least expensive.

Some colours will fade in bright sunlight (known as fugitive).

The tube, wrapping or colour chart will show the degree of permanency.

> **TIP**
> When pan-paint is running low, it is more difficult to load the brush with colour. A top-up of the same colour squeezed from a tube will revive the pan.

## Basic nature

*Pan paints will provide rich, dark colours*, as long as the swiftly dissoluble Artists' Quality colours are used. However, pan paints cannot equal the tube paints for producing large quantities of washes. Their strength instead lies in the instant availability of a range of colours within a single wash. Artists tend to build up their own range of colours, to suit their individual needs.

The manner in which pan paints are prepared for use can also make all the difference in getting the most out of them. Individually purchased pans are better stored in a special pan–paint box. This does however require that the wrapping is removed, which features all of the information relevant to that colour, as well as its name. Once the unwrapped pans are in use, it can become quite difficult to identify their colour, especially in the darker pigments. By fixing the wrappers to a section of the paint box, or a separate piece of card, in an order that matches the pans in the box, a useful colour chart is created for easy reference. This will reduce the likelihood of the wrong colour being picked up on the brush, which can have frustrating consequences. Another option is to make up a colour chart of small squares of painted colour in the relevant order, with the names written beside them.

*ARTSTRIPS©*

All watercolour paints lighten and become a little duller as they dry. This needs to be taken into account throughout the painting.

The transparency of the paint enables colours to be overlaid and mixed on the painting surface.

# Paints in practice
## Tube paints

*This exercise demonstrates* how light and depth is evoked by creating varying tone, rather than through the use of colour. Only one tube colour (Burnt Umber) is used to create varying tones (lights and darks) with washes and brush-strokes. Using a specific tube colour in this way, cuts out the need to deal with colour mixing, so that you can concentrate on the quality of the paint, the consistency of the washes and the strokes you make with the brush. Any subject will respond well to this treatment.

## Pan paints

As a complete contrast this study comprises a tapestry of small strokes, mixed from pan paints. Almost every stroke is a slightly different colour from the last. Either the colour has been changed, or another colour plus water has been added. These strokes could have been merged with one another, simply by increasing their proximity. However, they have been kept separate in order for you to observe the colour changes as they occur.

# Basic nature

Watercolour paint becomes lighter as it dries. Just when you think you have the painting right [A], it fades before your very eyes [B].

To achieve the right amount of drama, the paint needs to be applied more aggressively [C]. Then, as it dries, it retains the sort of contrasts that are needed [D].

# Positive layering

*Positive build up of colour* is when layers of transparent paint are laid on top of each other and thus mix on the surface. In each case the colours in the squares are the colours used in the layering in any particular area of painting and the position of the overlays matches the order in which the layers of colour lie.

Within each area of painting the set of colours have been graduated by adding water to each colour. As it is impossible to match the graduations in each set of colours, sometimes one colour will dominate in one place, while another will dominate elsewhere - producing an irregular patina.

This irregular mixing of paint in separate surface layers is quite different from the effect achieved through paint mixed on a palette. A palette mix would be more even and far less interesting.

Such layering would be limited were the paints naturally opaque, or if white was added to the colour.

# Exercise for paints

### NEGATIVE LAYERING

*Layers of mask are exploited*, in conjunction with layers of paint, in this unusual layering technique; where the positive strokes are produced through selective masking out on individual layers. In effect the paint is applied as negative layers through which the positive strokes will finally be revealed.

In this exercise the paint is built up in four layers -

Yellow [Yo+yg]

Orange [Yo+ro]

Brown ([Yo+ro] plus [bp])

Blue [Bp+bg]

The background is simply laid flat and as can be seen, more than three layers of paint and the colour does begin to texturize. In this case the texture adds character, but any further layers and the painting would certainly become 'dirty'. It could possibly also begin to damage - through unwanted paint lift.

Inside the glass objects the washes are graduated by losing edges - i.e. in some areas the brown is weaker than in others.

The main structure of the glass and stoppers (all the hard-edged strokes) is formed through the use of masking fluid on specific layers.

The white strokes are achieved through masking fluid applied to the bare paper. The yellow strokes are achieved through masking fluid applied to the yellow layer, once it had dried and so on.

When the mask is removed, the underlying three layers of colour and their mixtures are revealed as coloured strokes.

# Why do I need a brush?

*Not such a silly question, when there are so many other methods of applying paint. You can use anything, from a piece of twig to your fingers. Paint can be sprayed, splashed, squirted, dripped, dropped, rolled, or dabbed with tissue and sponge.*

**THERE IS NOTHING** wrong with any of these methods and all of them can be employed for explicit tasks and effects. In fact, the earliest brushes were probably twigs, with one end crushed into filaments.

Since those early days however, brushes have become increasingly sophisticated. But, along with sophistication, comes a proliferation of shapes and materials. To decide which is more suitable for you, it is better to return to basics and look at what the most common shapes do best. Along with this, it is essential to know what the brushes should be made of and why.

Many who start off with the wrong brush blame themselves for their inability to use it properly. This is perfectly natural. If you are trying to make a brush do something that it wasn't designed for, you are inevitably heading for disaster.

In the following section, we look at four basic brush shapes. The *Hake*, the *Round* brush, the *Flat* brush and the *Rigger*. These brushes are all one really needs to achieve professional results. Once you have a sound grounding and understanding of them, you will also have acquired the confidence with which to experiment with others.

> TIPS:
>
> • Always clean brushes at the end of a painting session.
>
> • When drying a brush out, stand it in a jar, never on its head.
>
> • Brushes made of natural hair must be protected against moth attack.

## COMMON TERMS

*In this book I have standardised the terms applied to the use of brushes, in order to make things simpler for those new to painting.*

*The handle of a brush* is known as the shaft. Traditionally made of wood with a sturdy coating, but plastic and other materials are also used these days.

*The hairs, or filaments,* that make up the brush head are set into a ferrule, the collar that holds the brush head to the shaft. The hairs are most likely to be set into the ferrule with glue, which can soften when warmed. Generally this ferrule is made from metal, although in some specialist brushes other materials are used.  Always wash brushes in cold or very tepid water, to prevent the metal ferrule from expanding and the glue softening, which would result in hairs falling out of the brush head.

*In round brushes and the Rigger,* the brush head makes two important contact points with the surface. The point being used for detail, while the side of the head – the shoulder – is employed for broader coverage.
*In the case of flat brushes,* the Hake and the flat wash brush, the tip of the brush is a long edge. The full edge is referred to as the tip, while one end of this edge is known as the corner of the tip. The flat surface of the brush head is termed the face of the brush.

*And finally, two terms that can cause some confusion.*

*A 'dry' brush* – obviously a brush needs to be wet in order to deliver paint to the surface. A brush becomes 'dry' when it has been deprived of fluid to the degree that when it is applied to the surface the paint does not flow, but will instead drag. Whether the paint is stiff, or fluid, it is the loading of the brush that is of importance here. The resultant stroke does not cover the paper completely and a scuff results. If the scuffs are repeated and merge together, creating an area of texture, this is known as a 'scumble'.

*A 'thirsty brush'* – when water or paint pools on the surface of the paper it can cause problems. This excess liquid therefore needs to be removed. Wet a brush and then gently squeeze out the liquid between fingers, or on an absorbent tissue. Never pull the hairs or this may damage them. The brush will now suck the liquid from the surface. Its natural ability to take up liquid makes it 'thirsty'.

# Understanding brushes

## Round brush

Features a round ferrule (metal collar). Round in cross-section. Most versatile shape of all brushes.

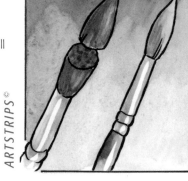

Point of head used for detail and shoulder (side) for broad coverage.

Loaded with dry mix, brush can be shaped on palette to produce line (point) or texture (shoulder).

## Hake brush

A wide flat brush. Features very soft goats hair. Shaft is unvarnished, light-weight wood.

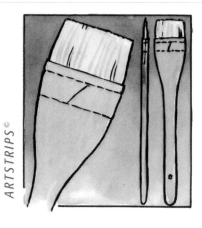

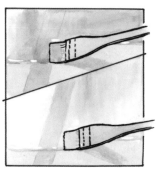

When new the head is quite bushy. Within a short time will develop a sharp edge.

Coverage – whether with colour or water – is swift and gentle. Essential for wet-on-wet over dried colour.

*The round brush* is the most popular and more importantly, the most versatile. Most sought after are those with the longest head and the finest point, for these offer control and the ability to paint detail. Brushes with natural hair, having filaments that naturally taper, offer the best points. Sable has the perfect balance of length and bounce and is thus the most highly respected. Since sable is expensive, other hair, such as squirrel or ox can be used, but none have the same characteristics.

Nylon, a modern equivalent, actually has more bounce, but less pointing and is more difficult to clean. Mixes of natural hair and nylon, or nylon alone suit many new to painting. As confidence grows, the move to sable will pay dividends.

*The Hake brush* is available in several forms and the finest, as usual, offers the better shaping and is lighter to the touch in use. Its secret is the goat hair in the head. This soft hair holds much fluid and can lay colour or water across an already painted surface, without causing any unwanted paint lift. It is therefore an essential brush for the Wet on Wet technique.

# Flat brush

Rectangular in cross-section, the ferrule being flat in shape. When wet, the tip has a sharp edge.

Heavy loading produces bold, even strokes. Light loading produces dry brushwork – (scuffing/scumbling).

Held at a sharp angle its aggressive edge can dissolve and lift paint layer.

*ARTSTRIPS©*

# Rigger brush

A 'stretched' round brush, with a fine point. The bigger the head, the more paint it will hold.

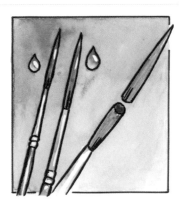

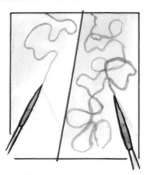

The flexible brush head provides fluid, loose linework.

Stroke it slowly – line is constant. Stroke it swiftly – line is broken (scuffed).

*ARTSTRIPS©*

*While both the flat and Rigger brushes* are available in natural hair, it is advisable to choose nylon in these instances. The flat brush, being mainly employed for paint lift, needs to be quite tough. Nylon is far more rugged than its natural counterpart and being cheaper, is far easier to replace.

*The fine tapering point of the Rigger* is easily distressed when composed of natural hair. The nylon Rigger has the advantage of that extra bounce inherent in its nylon filaments. This returns it to its natural shape more successfully.

*While, for all brushes, there are many variations* in head and shaft composition, shape and length, these are the basic collection of brushes you will need.

Certainly it is worth experimenting with different brushes when you find them, for that is the way in which artists discover their own particular styles. However, this basic collection of four brushes will serve you well for many years.

> **SIZING**
> As sizes vary across all manufacturers, it is not feasible to quote specifics. Whatever size you think you will need, always go for one two sizes larger, as smaller sizes seldom hold enough paint.

# Brushes in practice
## Hake brush

*The Hake brush* comes into its own for wetting either the paper surface, or the surface of a painted area, without disturbing the paint.

For this exercise using the Wet on Wet technique, a medium round brush is used to apply the colours, the Hake is kept purely for wetting the surface.

• The whole paper surface is wetted and the distant blue mountains painted in. This is left to dry thoroughly.

• Once dried through, the whole surface is wetted, including the previously painted area and the middle purple mountains painted in. Again, left to dry thoroughly.

• Once dried through, the whole surface is wetted, including the previously painted areas and the foreground green grey hills painted in.

Even though these layers were rewet more than once, the gentle nature of the Hake brush caused no disturbance of the paint.

**TOP ROW [Left to Right]**
Wet-on-wet brush-strokes, using the brush shoulder, with varying pressures.

Lost edges, using the shoulder of a second round brush.

Scuffs, using the brush shoulder.

**BOTTOM ROW [Left to Right]**
Directional strokes, using the brush tip.

Scumbles, using the brush shoulder.

Linework, using the brush point.

Masked linework, using the brush point, with overpainted solid wash.

## Round brush

The versatility of the round brush knows no bounds and is the mainstay of any painting kit. It is astonishing what can be achieved with just one brush and here we can see a small range of differing strokes achieved using a single, medium sized brush.

## Flat nylon brush

*The tip of* a medium flat nylon brush is used to lift off a heavy layer of watercolour from the surface, bit by bit, to create the image of the shell. The process is gradual, wetting only a few brushstrokes at a time before dabbing off with an absorbent tissue. The degree of white that can be attained depends mainly on the absorbency of the watercolour paper. However, it does depend to some extent on the staining power of the paint used. Nevertheless, the soft highlights produced can look very light against the darker colour.

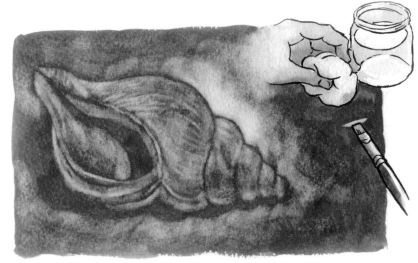

## Nylon rigger brush

*After an initial* gentle pencil drawing, stiff, wet-on-wet washes are applied using a round brush. These soft colours will not interfere with the linework to be drawn with a Rigger. The colour of the line, being watercolour, lightens as it dries, so should be tested for strength before applying to the subject. Also, being watercolour, the density of the line varies with the speed of application, as it does with the addition of more of the same colour, or others. The petal veins have more water added to the mix to make them lighter, but note that as the mix becomes more fluid the line does tend to widen slightly as the brush head swells.

# Exercise for brushes

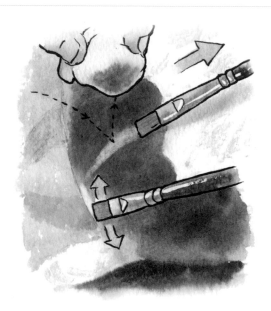

**Hake** Filled with a liquid mix, the Hake enables us to swiftly cover an area with a wash of colour. The edge of the brush tip gets efficiently into corners. Further on however, once the masking fluid is removed, a less generously loaded Hake is used to scuff colour on (blue over the snow). For this technique, the brush is drawn swiftly across the surface, merely tickling it.

**Flat Nylon** Lift-Off. Dark orange brown is blocked over the stone and post below it, using a large round brush. Once thoroughly dried the process of lift-off can be carried out. First, stroke the surface with a wet, flat nylon brush, using the face and dab off the colour with an absorbent tissue [top]. For more intensive linework, work the brush tip over the surface more vigorously before dabbing off [bottom].

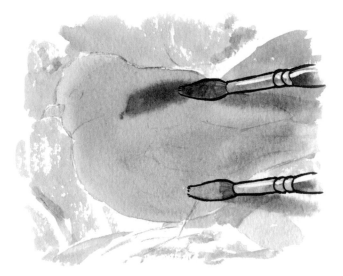

**Large & Medium Round Brushes** Wet the whole of the bird using the shoulder of a large round brush, then stroke in light washes [bottom] – warm orange on the front, cool orange greys at the back. While this is still wet, stroke in stiffer colours (dark browns) for the wing and head feathers [top].

**Rigger Brush** Linework with the Rigger tip completes the study by introducing a final touch of drawing, which pulls the shapes together. It also adds a dark accent against which the other colours can shine. Variations of pressure allow the line to describe the forms. Colour and the strengths of colour are varied likewise.

**This loose exercise** will enable you to not only employ a variety of brushes, but will give you the first chance to try painting with the Hake brush. After drawing in the composition, some masking is necessary, which is carried out with a large round brush throughout. Since this masked area is to be representative of snow on the leaves and the rock, avoid over heavy strokes in favour of using light scuffed strokes. This will suggest the texture of the snow and the play of light across the ice particles of its surface. Flatten the large round brush shoulder on the bed of the saucer palette as you sparingly load the masking fluid. As soon as the background washes are laid with the Hake and have dried, the masking fluid can be removed using a kneadable putty rubber.

*One final, but important piece of masking* – a tiny dot within the birds eye, without which this little dark spot would otherwise be lifeless.

# Why do I need a palette?

*The answer seems simple enough —
something on which to mix paint.
However, the palette offers much
more. When fully exploited it opens
up a multitude of possibilities that will
definitely enrich your painting.*

*This simple piece of equipment is as important a tool
as your brushes and paints. For not only does it provide a surface
on which to mix a spectrum of colours, it also provides the where-
withal to control the way paint is applied to the painting surface.*

*Many who are new to painting* use a large plate as their palette. This is
quite reasonable, for the plate does possess two of the important
requisites for a palette - it is waterproof and can be easily cleaned.
However, a plate does not measure up to the real purposes served by
the correct palette.

To begin with, your palette must offer suitable storage area for
paint squeezed from the tube, or in pans - one where the paint will be
reasonably safe from contamination by other colours. You will need to
control not only the placement of the paint, but also its fluidity. If it
becomes too dry it may take too long to dissolve. Too wet and it could
migrate around your palette.

Your palette must feature a good mixing area, one which makes the
paint easy to control during the mixing process. There are times when
these mixes need to be very fluid and others when they need to be
stiffer.

The versatility offered by selecting a suitable palette is invaluable.
How, for instance, would you change a colour gradually, in order to
achieve exactly the correct result? How will you mix just the right
amount to prevent yourself from running out of colour, or wasting it
by mixing too much?

With the right palette, one colour can be changed in three or more different ways, without losing the first mix.

Against this, a large plate does not come up to par, as mixed colours blur into one another and paint deposits dry up. In frustration you will wash away much good paint. Not only an unnecessary waste of paint, but more importantly, of your time and inevitably, loss of confidence.

## A GOOD PALETTE IS MADE FOR THE JOB.

The confusion facing artists is what to choose from the wide variety of available shapes and sizes. This section covers some of the basic shapes. By understanding how these work best, you will have a better understanding of the function of the many others that are produced by different manufacturers.

As you progress and find an area of watercolour in which you prefer to work, inevitably you will arrive at the palette, or palettes, with which you feel most comfortable.

For my part, I find the plastic rectangular Wet on Wet palette to be the most versatile. The largest size being my choice, for it provides the larger mixing area, along with the need to clean it less frequently. This not only saves on time, but also on colour mixes, to which I may return during the course of my painting.

Large palettes usually feature more paint wells, allowing for an increase in the colour range being squeezed out for use.

---

**TIP**:
When using a plastic palette for the first time, you are likely to find that the plastic surface repels the paint. This makes mixes difficult to assess since the paint does not spread, but collects in little globules over the surface.

To overcome this, use a clean paper tissue to spread a little Ox Gall or liquid household soap across the surface. These are water tension breakers and help to spread the liquid paint.

In the long run - make sure not to over wet the surface each time you wipe the palette clean. Better to rub the colour across the entire palette surface as you clean it with your absorbent tissue. This has the effect of spreading a thin layer of gum from the paint across the plastic and the paint mixes will spread much more easily in the future.

# Understanding palettes

## Wet on Dry palette

WELLED
RECTANGULAR
PALETTE. Ceramic or
plastic. Round wells
take tube paint.
Rectangular sloping
wells for large washes
of mixed colour.

ROUND WELLS. Moat of water
around mound of paint so it
stays wet.
RECTANGULAR WELLS. Sloped
floor and lip - useful for reducing
paint load in brush head.

NOTE Generous washes in wells
look dark. Test on piece of paper
to check value before using.

## Saucer palette

ROUND, SECTIONED
WELLS PALETTE.
Ceramic or plastic.
Ideal for small
amounts of fluid.
Example shows three
different solutions of
the same colour.

Ideal as temporary rest for brush
head full of colour.

Curved sides are useful for
removing excess fluid.

*Watercolour palettes are made in a variety of materials,* most commonly ceramic and plastic, with metal being another of the available options. Some artists even use natural objects, such as sea shells.

Metal watercolour palettes are lightweight and less likely to break. However, they are not a particularly pleasant surface on which to mix, unless the metal has been enamelled.

Watercolour palettes made from plastic are also lightweight, as you would expect, which makes this the ideal material for the large Wet on Wet palette. Unfortunately, plastic can stain, most notably when using paints made from strong dyes and/or when using inks for Line and Wash painting – although this is only a cosmetic problem.

*Other than for the plastic palette,* best suited for Wet on Wet watercolour painting, ceramic is preferable for both the Wet on Dry palette and the saucer palette. Both of which can be used with stronger paints and mediums, such as acrylics. The rectangular welled palette, is probably the most familiar shape, but, as shown, is designed to do a specific job. Struggling to make it work for Wet on Wet painting will lead only to frustration. Understanding what a specific palette can, or cannot do, is an integral part of painting and it is eventually well worth having all of the four palettes described in the Artstrips - in order to get the most from your paints.

## Wet on Wet palette

FLAT PLASTIC PALETTE. Round wells for ample paint storage. Large flat area – excellent for mixing.

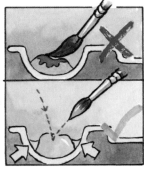

Loaded brush touching dry paint will deposit colour. Paint softened with moat of water is less likely to become tainted.

Large mixing area enables mixes to be developed. Hold brush at flat angle to make loading easier..

## Paint Box palette

Many paint boxes (plastic or metal) feature integral palette – in lid.

Can hold quite large washes. Three primary washes are often useful to begin a painting. But...

...much smaller quantities can also be mixed and colour change rapidly achieved. A real feature of these palettes.

*There are different versions* of the flat Wet on Wet watercolour palette. While it is preferable to have the central area completely flat, some versions are split into smaller compartments and there are those who find this a useful method for separating different washes. As long as you can get the brush down to a flat enough angle to mix and lift the paint, then the compartmentalised version will do the job.

When painting out of doors, many prefer to use a paint box. Most feature a secure method of holding the box, such as a finger loop, which means that both paints and palette are at hand. In spite of the fact that the paint box palette, by its very nature, does not deliver vast amounts of colour swiftly, it is very versatile - provided you do not want to work on too large a scale.

Some artists do not like to use these palettes, for the enamel tends to discolour. Personally, however, I find the appearance of an old, well-used paint box, a joy to behold, as it tells of many happy hours spent painting.

# Palettes in practice
## Wet on Dry palette

*The welled, rectangular* palette is best employed for large washes of flat or graded colour. The larger the area to be painted, the larger the brush needed. The purity of these clear thin washes shows watercolour at its best.

> Each palette shape has its unique specialities or functions for the techniques to which it is best suited

## Saucer palette

*The round saucer* palette holds small, or even tiny, amounts of fluid. Small brushes and Riggers work well with it. In this example the wells contain three different strengths of Indian ink used to produce the silhouette linework, or drawing, which is progressively lightened to suggest distance. Next, the wells are filled with thin colours for the small washes, or coloured hatching, used to solidify the form.

**NOTE**
The white hatched strokes. These are placed in the same manner using masking fluid, to protect the paper before colour is applied. Once removed the white strokes are revealed.

## Wet on Wet palette

*By far the most* versatile, the Wet on Wet palette really comes into its own for mixing the stiff, tube colours, required for painting wet-into-wet. It nestles comfortably in the crook of the arm and several brushes can be supported in the finger hold, making it an excellent choice for working out of doors.

## Paint Box palette

*A good choice* for producing smaller work when working outside. Look for those that have some form of finger or hand hold, which makes the paint box easy to support while standing. In this example you can see the main strength of the paint box palette – enabling rapid colour change, either between small washes (background) or within very tiny areas (flowers and leaf). The pans of paint provide a far greater range of immediately accessible colours.

# Exercise for palettes

**Colour Mix using the Wet on Dry palette** Start the large background wash with a fluid mix of cool grey blue ([Bp] plus [yo+ro]). Apply with a large round brush, which will cover swiftly, while providing a point for working into corners. Add water and thoroughly mix the solution as you move downward.

**Colour Mix using the Wet on Wet palette** Mix a strong cool grey green ([Bg+Yo] plus [ro]). Wet the surface of the painting broadly right across leaf edges. Apply with a medium sized round brush following the 'flow' of each leaf.

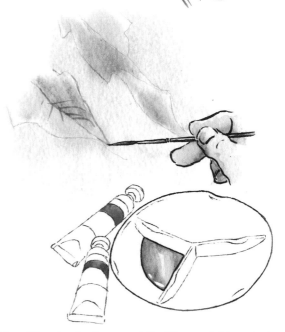

**Colour Mix using the Paint Box palette** Produce three small quantities of rich red - 1. [Ro] 2. [Ro+Rp] 3. [Ro+Rp+bp] Use a small round brush and change the mix frequently as you note the differences of value in the subject.

**Colour Mix using the Saucer palette** Mix a small thin wash of grey green [Bp+Yo+ro]. Starting at the bottom, use a Rigger brush to redraw the silhouette and the leaf veins with a fluid line. Vary the line colour by adding [Ro] and [Rp] (no added water) as you move up the painting.

**Seldom would you** use the set of four different palettes when working on one painting. However, as an exercise, this will teach you a great deal about the relative strengths of each and offer some insight as to which to utilise for specific requirements.

The finished study is principally a Line & Wash painting. Note how the line itself moves from strong red at the top, to a gentle grey-green at the base.

Whenever you paint plants or flowers, it is important to be selective about what you are going to paint from the vast range of detail within the subject matter. Here the flow of the line across and around the form of the leaves traces their rhythms and movements. Like a spider's web, it holds together the many different types of brush stroke and colour mix employed throughout the piece.

# What is so special about watercolour paper?

*The answer is simple - Watercolour paper is special. So much so that, should you not be using it or, if using the wrong type, no matter how well the techniques of watercolour painting have been mastered, you will run into trouble.*

*I have myself fallen foul of this potential problem* on an occasion when carrying out a live demonstration. The point was reached when I needed to make corrections. With a confident smile I explained that watercolour paint can easily be removed, either to correct mistakes or to produce soft highlights.

Having introduced the correct brush to use and talked about what was going to happen I applied my brush to the surface. Immediately it became obvious that something was wrong – the colour refused to move. More pressure was applied and still nothing. My mind raced, there had to be a simple explanation.

Of course there was! The paper purchased on the previous day was not what I thought it was. I had been in too much of a hurry to check the paper in the store and the stock on the shelves must have been moved. The paper being used was producing wonderful washes, with some terrific textures and so it should, for it was a very absorbent paper. As a result, the colour was travelling deep into the paper surface and the only thing that could possibly have shifted the paint was to rub it out with sandpaper

Selecting the right paper is just important as getting the correct brush or choosing the most suitable paint. When starting out in water-colour painting, it is far better to avoid potential problems that would undoubtedly prove disheartening.

It is not possible to successfully master techniques on anything other than watercolour paper, which has been developed specifically to do the job.

> **TIP**:
>
> Many manufacturers produce sample pouches containing different surface and weights of paper on which to experiment. To test out paper samples, try different techniques and mediums i.e. a wash, a graded wash, losing edges, wet-on-wet, lift off and masking fluid.
>
> You will be surprised at the differences across the types of paper.
>
> Keep these test samples for future reference.

As you will soon discover, there are many types of watercolour paper - some cheaper than others.  As with all painting tools, it is important to understand the differences, in order to make an informed choice as to which to use, to achieve the result being sought.

Principally what are their main strengths and weaknesses - for instance, the previously mentioned absorbent paper? Although it did not yield the desired result, it was nevertheless not a bad paper. Simply that it was not suitable for the technique being demonstrated. Had its characteristics been matched and masking fluid been applied to protect the highlights and areas for the gentle washes, then it would have been an unqualified success.

## SELECTING YOUR SURFACES

*It is precisely for this reason* that it is not possible to simply suggest one paper over another, as being suitable for every painting and a cure-all to protect against every potential problem. It is up to the individual to experiment with different surfaces from which to arrive at a decision as to which suits best.

Many starting out in watercolour painting tend to opt for a NOT paper to begin with. While these are textured, they are not overly so and the texture will vary dramatically between the different types. Some have very regular textures (lines, diagonals, patterns), others are more amorphous.

Expense does come into play when choosing papers. It does not make sense when starting out to select a hand-made, tub sized cotton paper. This is the top of the rouge and you are likely to be terrified to make a mark on the surface.

Far better to start with students' quality, for you are more likely to make progress by allowing yourself the freedom to make mistakes on a cheaper paper. As your confidence grows, move up the scale to enjoy the unbeatable qualities of the best watercolour papers.

# Understanding surfaces

## Watercolour paper

Watercolour paper is available in different weights (thicknesses) [top] and in differing textures [bottom].

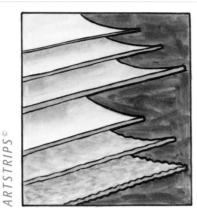

The thinner the paper, the more it will distort when wet. Important - different watercolour techniques demand different wettings.

## Basic types

Water is drained from fibres in solution to make the natural textured surface of ROUGH paper.

While wet, the rough paper can be hot rolled and becomes smooth - HOT PRESSED or HP

Or it can be rolled cold - COLD PRESSED, CP or NOT (is not hot pressed).

*Buying watercolour paper in sheets* is by far the most economical, against the added costs of pre-cut paper bound into pads or blocks. However, pads and blocks can be more practical in many instances, such as painting out and about, or when taking your equipment to classes.

The thinner, lighter weight papers - 200gsm (90lb), are better suited to working on a smaller scale and with the gentlest of watercolour sketches, which require little wetting. Medium weight papers - 300gsm (140lb), are ideal for practise work and general usage. While the heavy weight papers of 425gsm (200lb), 600gsm (300lb) and upwards come into their own for more professional work.

*Watercolour pads and blocks* come in all shapes and sizes, but it is essential to establish of what type and weight of paper they comprise. It does not necessarily follow that the paper in a pad stated as containing watercolour paper, will be suitable for every type of watercolour painting. Spiral bound pads are better, as the remaining sheets are more likely to stay in place when a sheet is torn out.

Blocks of watercolour paper are useful, especially when travelling, as the sheets are fixed along their edges. In spite of this the paper is not stretched and therefore is still prone to cockling.

## Basic qualities

 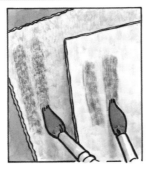  

The smooth HP papers are excellent for line-work and detail, but their surfaces can be weak from being pressed during manufacture.

NOT and ROUGH have more texture to be exploited.

BASIC NATURE - All water-colour papers contain size. The amount can vary and this affects absorbency and strength.

ONCE MADE - Extra size can be added by dipping sheet into tub of size and redrying (TUB SIZING).

## Basic forms

Papers are available in sheets. Many have a right and wrong side. Watermark reads on the right side.

When cutting up sheets, mark the corners of the correct side with a pencil as a reminder.

Paper is also available in pads (use spiral bound) and blocks (paper glued at edges). The right side faces upward.

*Any watercolour paper* under 425gsm (200lb) really needs to be stretched on a board, to remain perfectly flat when painting. Although thick sheets may not ripple when wet, they do buckle or bend into large waves that make them difficult to mount when framing.

The theory behind stretching paper is simple. When the paper is wet its fibres expand and consequently the paper expands. Should the paper be fixed along all of its edges while in this wet state, once dried out it shrinks and becomes taut like the stretched skin of a drum.

*This stretched paper* is less likely to wrinkle if rewet, especially if only a portion of the paper is wetted, which is usual in the painting process. If the paper stretched does wrinkle, then at least it will flatten out again on drying, leaving a perfectly level piece of finished artwork.

The paper only remains stretched as long as its edges remain fixed. Once the paper edges are released the paper will return to its normal size, as the paper is no longer stretched.

# Surfaces in practice

## Stretching paper for watercolours

**1.** *When any sheet of paper* is dampened its fibres absorb the water and it stretches or expands. As the water evaporates, the fibres and thus the whole sheet, shrink back to their former size.

**2.** *The thicker the paper*, the more water and soaking time is required to stretch it. With 200gsm to 300gsm (90 to 140lb) weights, simply wet both sides with a soft (natural) sponge. It is important to ensure the wrong side is wetted first, as this may pick up dirt or stains from the drawing board, when you turn it over to wet the second side.

With 300gsm to 425gsm (140 to 200lb) weights, you can run both sides under a tap. Leave 425gsm to 600gsm (200 to 300lb) papers in a bath of cold water for approximately five minutes - stretch a few pieces on separate boards to make it worth your while filling a bath with water.

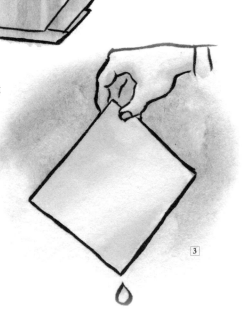

**3.** *Really wet papers* need to be lifted gently by one corner, avoiding folding or bending. Allow sufficient time for excess water to run off. Then turn the paper to hold it by its opposite corner so that the water on the sheet will not be concentrated in one corner, but evenly distributed.

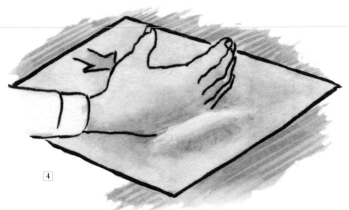

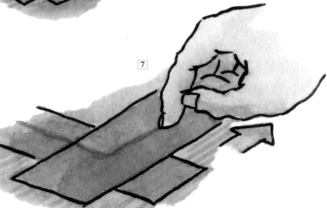

**4.** *Transfer the sheet to a drawing board*, which should be unvarnished plain wood of a sufficient thickness not to bend under the strain of the stretching paper (hardboard will not do). Excessive bubbles of air can be gently squeezed out with the side of your hand.

**TIP**

A drawing board for stretching paper can be expensive. A sheet of 12mm (1/2") plywood will do, cut to size and sanded smooth on all four edges and both faces. To allow for the gum strip overlap the board should be 50mm (2") larger in each dimension than the size of paper most commonly used.

**5.** *The paper is now to be fixed* along its edges with 50mm (2") wide gum strip - a gummed paper parcel tape that has water-soluble gum on the reverse. Rolls of gum strip must never come into contact with water or the whole roll with stick together.
To avoid this, pre-cut lengths at least 50mm (2") longer than the length of the paper - four pieces in all, before you begin working with the wet paper. Each length should be immersed in water and then run between two fingers to remove excess moisture.

**6.** *Lay the gum strip* along the edge of the paper half on the paper and half on the board. Holding down one corner of the gum strip, press down firmly with a tissue. Run the tissue firmly along the length of gum strip, overlapping its paper edge. Excess 'gummy' water will be squeezed out onto the paper and this needs to be picked up on the tissue before it can spread.

**7.** *As a final seal*, run your fingernail along the ridge formed at the paper's edge beneath the gum strip.

# Exercise for surfaces
## Surface textures

The surface texture of watercolour paper can be exploited in many ways. This exercise is produced using cold candle wax as a resist, sgraffito to create textured strokes, knifing out to create textured highlights and impasto medium to thicken the paint.

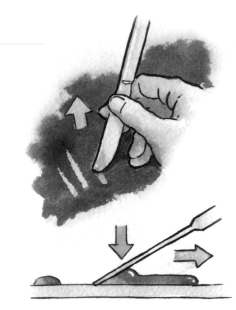

**Candle wax** - Carefully split a candle lengthways. Lay graded bright washes over the sky, mountain and water. Judiciously draw the candle wax on the surface. It is difficult to see the deposit of wax, unless you lift the surface up to the light and look along the surface. Now paint over the candle wax with another layer of graded colour and note how the wax resist picks out the surface texture of the paper. Try with different papers and varying degrees of texture to explore all the possibilities of this unusual technique.

**Knifing out** - This techniques requires a blunt eating knife - sharp edges would damage the paper. The idea behind this technique is to squeeze the colour from the surface, before it has had time to dry. This technique is known as knifing out. Start by wetting the area and laying a large area of heavy colour. Take the blunt knifepoint and at a shallow angle, apply pressure to it while pulling the blade across the surface. Too high an angle and you may tear the wet paper. The colour will be squeezed out and if you ease the pressure toward the end of the stroke the resultant mark will thin out. Timing is all-important and results are better just before the wash begins to dry - you only find out by trying a test stroke.

**Sgraffito** - Lay washes over the water and before it has had time to dry, reverse the brush in your hand and scratch the surface (sgraffito) to suggest reeds and grasses growing from the water surface. Each scratch damages the paper and it begins to absorb the colour more swiftly than the paper surface all around. When the second wash is applied these marks will simply get darker. While this is a rewarding technique, you will need to take into account that these marks are permanent. Do not be frightened off using this technique - just carefully consider where you are going to make the scratches. It is the fluidity of the line that is more important, rather than absolute accuracy.

**Impasto medium** - Instead of using the surface, this technique requires the addition of a medium to create a totally different type of surface. The medium concerned is watercolour impasto medium, which is available in a tube. It is a transparent medium, to which watercolour can be added to achieve a buttery consistency. First the foreground is given an orange brown wash. When dry, the impasto colour is laid freely on the right hand side, using an oil painters painting knife. For the left hand side, rewet the surface and boldly brush on an orange impasto mix, using a large round brush. Before this dries, use the brush shaft to gently scratch through the thick layer. Finally, use a Rigger brush to drop on flecks of a darker impasto mix on grass or reed heads.

# Why bother with colour mixing?

After all, most watercolour paint ranges seem to offer virtually every colour, some feature forty or more.

*There is absolutely nothing wrong in having as large a colour range as you wish. Every artist develops their own palette of preferred colours, but to arrive at this selection requires knowledge of not only the available colours, but how colours work with each other to produce successful mixes.*

**COLOUR MIXING** is every bit as important in making a composition work as perspective or drawing. With colour control you can communicate with the viewer, tell a story or evoke a mood – hence the phrase 'to paint a picture'.

It is important to think of colours as more than just the names that appear on the tube or pan, which in themselves can be confusing as they are not necessarily standard across the various manufacturers. What matters is the colour itself and where it is positioned on the colour wheel. This may at first seem a little complex, but in reality it is relatively simple and only requires thinking through and practice.

Once the colour circle and the position of the paints on it have been mastered, the potential for controlled colour mixing will be fully appreciated. This control will allow you to not only reproduce any particular colour, but also to control the balance of colour across the whole of the painting's surface.

The character of watercolour paintings is dominated by its transparency. More than any other medium this must be made to work and you need to know which paints and mixes will achieve this. You also need to understand how many layers of a specific colour can be applied.

To make the transition from understanding colour mixing, to putting it into practice, you need to know how to physically mix colours on the palette and on the painting surface.

| COLOUR REFERENCE | COLOUR MIXING |
|---|---|
| Red-purple [Rp]<br>Red-orange [Ro]<br>Blue-purple [Bp]<br>Blue-green [Bg]<br>Yellow-orange [Yo]<br>Yellow-green [Yg] | Where the pre-fix letter is shown in capitals this denotes a larger quantity of that particular colour.<br><br>Conversely, where the pre-fix letter is shown in a lower case, this denotes a smaller quantity of that particular colour.<br><br>Example:<br>Bp = **large** amount of blue-purple<br>bp = **small** amount of blue-purple |

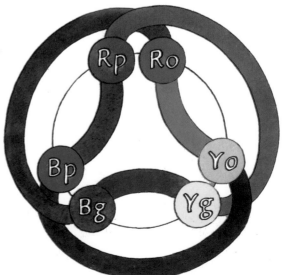

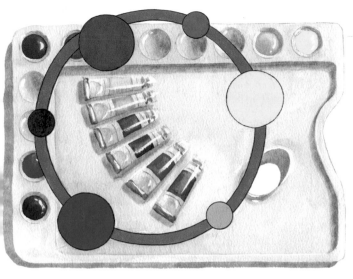

Every colour has a different tinting strength, which has nothing to do with its position on the colour circle. It is merely that with some colours a lot of paint is required and with others, less is needed. This knowledge can only be acquired through practising colour mixing on the palette.

Simplicity is the essence of good watercolour techniques. A surface that becomes overworked becomes dirty and unpleasant. You need to learn how to avoid such dirty colour mixes and should they occur, how to repair or replace them.

Once that knowledge has been acquired it becomes obvious that working with watercolours makes certain demands, which force you to be sensible with the number of colours you use. If there were forty in your palette, think of the inconvenience of dealing with all those tubes or pans.

No palette would be large enough to take the extensive range that would be required to complete any one painting, much less the whole set. Some colours would need replenishing more frequently, an unwelcome interruption to the workflow. A range of forty pans is not inconceivable, but think of the confusion when searching out a particular colour.

Learning the theory and practical aspects of colour mixing is thus essential for the future enjoyment of painting in watercolours. Not only does mixing colours become a pleasure, it will affect your observation of everything that is going on around you. The world out there is full of colour and it is waiting to be discovered and painted by you.

## SETTING OUT A PALETTE

For ease of reference, it is far better to arrange the paints in the palettes to reflect their position on the colour circle. For the Wet on Wet, plastic rectangular palette, squeeze the primary colours into the wells positioned at the three corners. Ensure these are placed so that matching biases are next to one another. Lay out the pan paint box in a similar manner.

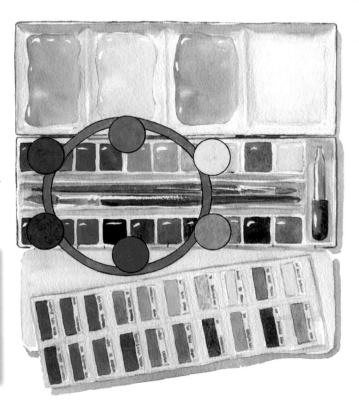

---

**TIP**:

When following the tuition in this book, rather than just accepting a suggested colour mix, consider what is behind that suggestion. Work out how the mix is functioning and if it does not happen the first time, resolve to find out why it failed. Just as much can be learnt from failures in colour mixing as can be from successes.

PRIMARY COLOURS cannot be achieved through mixing. Instead are used in mixes to achieve other colours.

In theory - primary colours are mixed to create secondary colours.

Sometimes this just does not seem to work, because...

...more than one set of primaries are required. Ones that are biased to the secondary colours they mix.

From which can be created bright secondaries...

...or dull secondaries.

For palette mixing these primaries are best laid out like the colour circle to make identification and mixing easier.

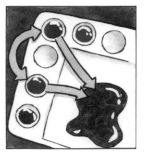

Mixing colours that are close produces bright secondary colours.

Mixing colours that are more distant produces dull secondary colours.

TAKE CARE : Some colours are more powerful in mixtures (tinting strength). Adding equal amounts does not always yield the expected result.

By adjusting quantities, a middle secondary is achieved.

Mixture is controlled by adding just a little of the strong colour to the edge of the weaker mix.

# Palette mixing

### BRIGHT SECONDARY MIXES

Mixing primaries next to one another on the colour circle creates intense (bright) secondary mixes.

Red-orange [Ro] +Yellow-orange [Yo] make a good orange, both having an orange bias.

The purple grapes are mixed from Red-purple [Rp] + Blue-purple [Bp].

The green of the apples, while both being mixed from Blue-green [Bg] + Yellow-green [Yg] appear to be different.

This simple change is made by adding more yellow to the fruit in the foreground and more blue to the one behind.

### DULL SECONDARY MIXES

These mixes are created by using primaries at the furthest distance from each other, with a bias away from the secondary colour for which they have been chosen to mix.

The orange is therefore mixed from Yellow-green [Yg] + Red-purple [Rp].

The grapes are Red-orange [Ro] + Blue-green [Bg], while the apples are a mix of Blue-purple [Bp] + Yellow-orange [Yo].

Again, the apples have either more yellow (front) or more blue (back) in their mix.

Note how grey the grapes have become and while the orange is probably the brightest of the mixes, compare it with the bright orange of close primaries in the first example.

# Exercise

## BRIGHT SECONDARY MIXES

The bottom half of this exercise is painted in all the bright secondary mixes. In the mixes shown, the first colour is the dominant colour in the final mix. In the diagram the differing sizes of the circles are used to indicate that the quantity of each pigment varies in line with the tinting strength of the paint used in the mix. For instance, in the blue green mix used for the trees, the amount of blue required is small. The tinting strength of the blue being so strong, that only a little was needed to achieve the required bias.

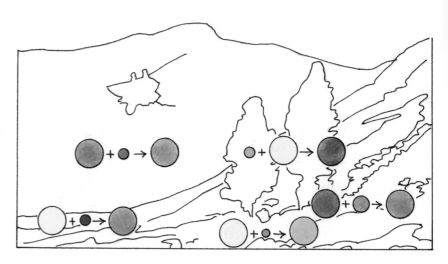

## DULL SECONDARY MIXES

The top half of the exercise is painted using dull secondary mixes, for which there is a greater range of choice as to which primary to employ. For instance - the purple mix for sky and distant hill, as opposed to the purple colour of the close headland. These are both mixed using red and blue. However, one mix features a blue-purple, while the other features a blue-green. Neither of these blues is exactly adjacent to red-orange. Their closest neighbour is red-purple. Blue-green, being the most distant from the red-orange, creates the dullest mix.

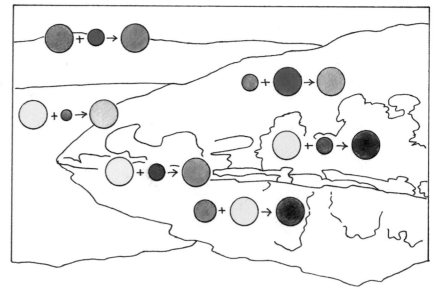

## NOTE

THE AMOUNT OF WATER IN THE MIX MAKES QUITE A DIFFERENCE. COMPARE THE MIX OF GREEN FOR THE DISTANT WATER AGAINST THE MIX FOR THE TREES, MIDDLE RIGHT.

This simple exercise is painted wet-on-wet, so that the resultant landscape is suggested, rather than rendered in detail. All of the colours used are created as secondary mixes, but those on the top half are dull, while those used for the bottom half are bright.

In spite of the fact that there are no strong value differences (light vs dark), the colours evoke a sense of depth and light. This is due to a phenomenon known as 'aerial perspective'. One aspect of this is that colours become duller (lose intensity) as they move into the distance. By changing to mixes that are naturally duller, for those far away hills, a sense of depth is created.

A real feeling for the range of mixes available to you can only be truly achieved through carrying out simple exercises such as this for yourself.

## REMINDER
ADD COLOUR TO A PALETTE MIX BY INTRODUCING IT FROM THE SIDE, RATHER THAN ADDING TO THE CENTRE. THIS ALLOWS FOR CONTROL OVER EXACTLY HOW MUCH OF EACH IS USED, WITHOUT MIXES GOING AWRY AND BECOMING INCREASINGLY LARGER.

# Common problems

**PROBLEM**

*It is easy, through overworking, or by mixing the wrong primaries, to end up with a duller (less intense) mix than expected. Just as frustratingly, watercolours become slightly duller as they dry. This is especially noticeable when rendering flowers. Purple flowers especially, can be extremely dark, yet still intense in hue.*

**MISTAKE**

**A** - Whilst blue-purple [Bp] is a good choice, since it has a bias towards purple, the red-orange [Ro] has a bias towards orange, resulting in the flower head being a little grey, not what is required.

**SOLUTION**

**B** - This can easily be overcome with a glaze of colour being overpainted. A glaze being produced either, with a primary, or with a bright secondary mix. In this example a darker mix than might be expected is used. Not only will this naturally dry lighter, but it will also sink into the colour beneath. As the two layers mix and dry, the top colour will appear to become more transparent.

**C** - Here the overlaid glaze comprises Blue-purple [Bp] + Red-purple [Rp].

**D** - As these two colours are neighbours on the colour circle, they share the same bias towards purple and are intense enough and dark enough to achieve the required effect.

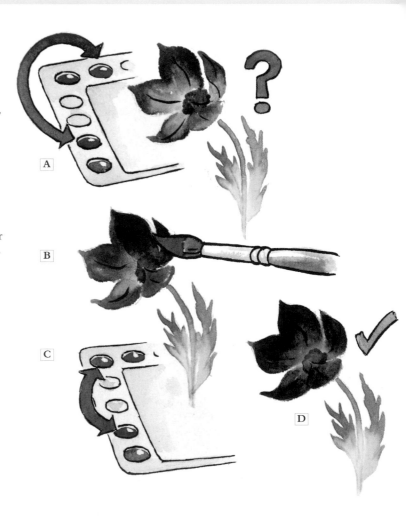

## NOTE

COLOURS CAN ALSO BE DULLED DOWN BY ADDING DULL COLOUR OVER INTENSE ONES. THIS HAPPENS LESS FREQUENTLY, BUT CAN, NEVERTHELESS, BE EFFECTIVE.

*Having glazed* with the most intense secondary possible, let us explore further possibilities through mixing these colours that are immediate neighbours on the colour circle and the palette.

### EXAMPLE

**A** - The base mix is the bright secondary purple, comprising Blue-purple [Bp] + Red-purple [Rp]. This mix can be made bluer, or more red, depending on the quantity of each colour used.

**B** - Frustratingly, these mixes are still not intense enough to match the intense coloration in the flower head. Although, compared to the previous example they are bright, as they contain no Red-orange [Ro].

For the first time, the basic palette of colours is just not sufficient. For in reality, whenever two colours are mixed, the result is always a little less intense than either of the original hues.

### SOLUTION

**C** - The only answer is to have additional tubes or pans of specific secondary colours. These are produced in as bright a hue as possible, far brighter than can be achieved through mixing.

### NOTE

IN THE ROW OF THREE FLOWERS, OBSERVE HOW IN SOME PLACES THE COLOURS HAVE STARTED TO SEPARATE, AS A RESULT OF THE MIX BECOMING RATHER FLUID. THIS IS REFERRED TO AS GRANULATION AND COULD BE USED AS AN EFFECT.

*ARTSTRIPS* ©

Paint can be held within one, or all, of three areas of a brush head. Tip (red). Shoulder (blue). Body (yellow).

A well-loaded brush will deliver a constant supply of colour to the tip.

If mix is uneven inside the brush head, delivery will be graduated.

To mix colour evenly inside the brush, the whole head must come into contact with the palette.

If only the tip is employed, then only colour in the tip will be mixed.

LOADING - After mixing, the brush should be angled low on the palette, so that the shoulder can absorb the colour.

DELIVERY - Every time a brush is lifted off the surface it creates a small pool of colour. This creates uneven washes.

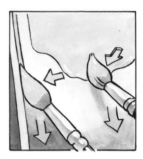

During a wash the brush should be kept under constant pressure on the paper to produce a more even layer of colour.

After applying wash, dip the brush in water without touching the sides or washing out the colour...

...return the brush to the clean palette surface to mix colour and water in the brush head (top). Continue wash with this lighter mix.

Load shoulder of brush with two different colour on each side...

...to create mixed colour strokes every time you touch the paper surface.

# Brush mixing

### BRUSH-HEAD MIXES

In this example, both mother duck and ducklings are painted mixing the colour in the brush head alone.

The adult and the two cool ducklings have progressively more water added to their mix, by dipping the brush in the water jar. Note the edges of the gradation, which are left quite pronounced, for two reasons. Firstly so that they can be seen in this example and secondly, because they also resemble the feather texture you would expect on a bird.  For more gradual change only dip the tip of the brush into the water and make more graduations. Colour changes for the warm duckling at the front is achieved by dipping the brush into a separate colour wash, pre-mixed on the palette, rather than clean water.

### MIXED COLOUR STROKE

It is very exciting to use a brush loaded with two colours at the same time. On the left, the tree is painted wet-on-dry; the brush shoulder loaded with yellow green and blue green on opposite sides. Every attempt is made to get the yellow green side facing the top of each stroke to suggest sunlight. Each stroke is different however, but this is part of the fun. Strokes are pulled from the outside of the tree toward the trunk.

The other two trees are painted wet-on-wet, the centre tree being painted in the same manner as its partner on the left, but showing different qualities due to the wet surface. To the right however, another colour, a warm brown, is added, so that the brush head is split into three colours. As the colour is laid, the brush is twisted to present different colours to the surface.

# Exercise

**BRUSH-HEAD MIX**

**Fig. A** - With a medium round brush the stroke is started at the top, loaded with a purple mix. The brush is then dipped into water and transferred to the clean palette and brush-head mixed. Eventually, a second, pre-mixed red is added, using a progression of further brush-head mixes. The angle of application to the paper is kept medium to low (top left) to ensure a smooth transition of colour.

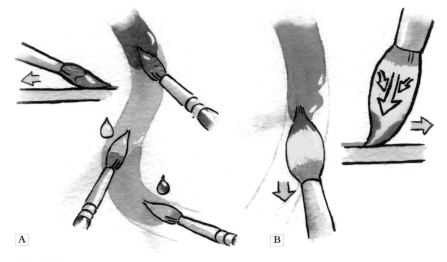

**TIP MIX**

**Fig. B** - A larger brush is first loaded generously with yellow. Pure red is tip mixed into its point, mixing to a deep orange. The brush is transferred to the surface and the angle of application (top right) is kept steep, so that all the painting is achieved with the tip. Only one loading is made and the colour changes as the yellow is pulled from the brush body, while it makes its journey down to the tail of the serpent.

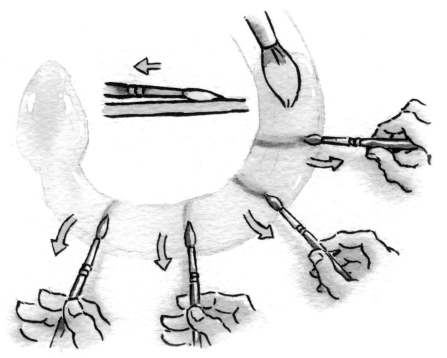

**TWO COLOUR STROKE**

The whole length of the painted area is first wetted with a large brush and later progressively rewetted, section by section as the painting continues. Two thick washes are mixed on the palette and the brush shoulder of a medium (to small) brush is loaded (blue green one side, blue the other). The brush angle is kept low (centre) as the strokes are applied wet-on-wet. Note the directional strokes and the volume that they suggest, also the unusual ways in which the brush is gripped, with the shaft being held both overhand and underhand.

*This coil of serpents* is not as intimidating as it looks. It offers not only a great exercise in brush mixing, but also one of brush control. You will be using three different sized brushes, all in unique ways.

## TIP MIXING:
### Orange to yellow

One loading of a large round brush will complete the snake. Mixing and painting with its tip is excellent practice for detailing through point control. The aim of this exercise is to produce a smooth transition of colour, so keep the brush in contact with the surface as much as possible during application.

## BRUSH-HEAD MIXING:
### Purple/Water/Red

This technique, using a medium size round brush, is probably the most important on the page, for you will not always want to mix vast quantities of colour. With small mixes, colour changes can be made rapidly, even over a small area. Note how the colour change in this exercise, as opposed to the example with the ducklings, is much smoother. This is achieved by adding only a touch of water, or later on, colour, and moving only a short distance with each change.

## TWO COLOUR STROKES:
### Blue and yellow green

Working wet-on-wet is always exciting and when combined with the directional strokes from a small round brush, is also effective. Practice using different fluidities of colour to experience the different colour flows and how they affect the final mix. Tidy up some edges of the snake body by flattening the brush on the palette and stroking in a fine line using its tip edge. The brush holds may seem a little awkward at first, but practice them and they will soon become second nature.

# Common problems

---

**PROBLEM**

*Graduated washes can go awry and could turn out unevenly, even for those with many years experience in watercolour painting [A]. After all, working with watercolours is all about letting the paint flow and seeing what happens when it dries. The result is always a surprise - often wonderful, but occasionally not so. Many things can affect the result. The atmosphere could be too dry, the mix in the brush might be wrong. Even the angle of the board that supports the work in progress will have a bearing. There is no need to despair, as the situation can be remedied.*

---

## DEALING WITH A WET SURFACE

When dealing with a wet surface, this corrective technique requires patient handling. It is worth it however to rescue the painting. However, the corrective process needs to be understood to be effective and this is only possible through experiencing the possible side effects of approaching the task with a heavy hand and in a hurry.

**B** - Avoid approaching the surface with a brush that is holding too much water. This could result in a back-run, where the water floods out, carrying the colour with it.

**C** - A lightly loaded damp brush could act like a thirsty brush, lifting the colour irregularly.

**D** - You might simply brush the colour too vigorously, resulting in a dirty, untidy appearance to what should have been a clean wash.

## SOLUTION

This technique is based on feathering the colour to achieve the desired even wash.

**E** - Gently squeeze a damp brush between you fingers to remove excess water and shape the brush into a fan.

**F** - Using the tip of the brush hairs, gently stroke over the offending irregular wash edge, thus delicately moving the particles of pigment into place.

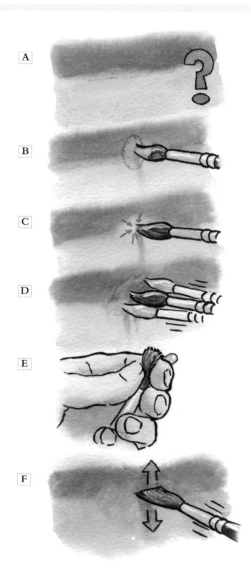

## DEALING WITH A DRY SURFACE

Time and atmosphere play such an important role in the drying of watercolour that there are no hard and fast rules. It is up to the individual to determine just how dry the surface really is. If it is too dry, the colour simply cannot be feathered. Should the surface be partly wet, only some of the colour can be moved and this may make matters worse.

Rather than risk it, far better to wait until the surface is totally dry. Either wait for the surface to dry completely, or speed things up by using a hairdryer.

The first approach is to carry out a gentle or partial lift of any area that is too dark.

**A** - With a large soft brush, gently lay water on the area concerned. Do not rub or work at the surface at all with the brush.

**B** - Quickly but gently dab the area with a smooth, absorbent tissue or paper towel. Again, do not move the tissue on the surface, but simply press it gently and evenly.

**C** - Lift the tissue and note how a small amount of colour will have been taken up by it.

This process should be repeated as many times as required. However, rather than run the risk of lifting off too much colour, it is advisable to ensure that the first wetting is completely dry, before attempting to rewet the area and lifting-off again.

## REPAIRING COLOUR

In the event that too much colour has been lifted off and needs to be repaired, this too can be resolved. There may also be occasions when colour needs to be added to a wash, in which case the following solution applies to both.

Make up a palette mix of the desired colour. Use a soft brush to gently lay water on the area in question, as in the method for lift-off.

**D** - In this instance however, as opposed to lifting colour, take some of the colour from your palette and gently slide it into the wetted area. Try not to disturb the colour beneath, by keeping the pressure of application gentle and presenting the brush at a shallow angle to the surface.

Allow to dry and if necessary, repeat the process.

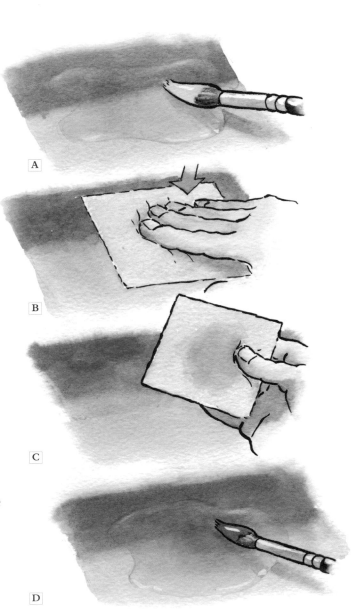

*ARTSTRIPS* ©

LAYER MIXING Lay a wash of colour and leave to dry thoroughly.

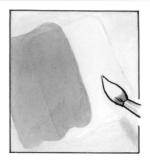

Lay a second colour so that it partly overlays the first, dry wash.

Keep the brushwork fast, simple and gentle, so as not to disturb underlying colour layer.

Up to three applications can be layered successfully. Beyond this it is difficult not to loosen and lift dry colour beneath.

LOSING INTO COLOUR Lay a fluid mix of colour onto a dry surface...

...then lay a second colour next to it. The colours are lost (flow) into one another and mix.

DRIP COLOUR MIX Use brush point to lay deep line of water across surface of a level, or gently angled, piece of paper.

Drip fluid colours into the water. The water tension carries the colours along the water and where colours meet they mix.

COMPLEMENTARY LAYER MIXING Lay a clean wash of red [Rp+Ro] across a piece of watercolour paper. Allow to dry thoroughly.

Gently lay a clean green wash [Yg+Bg] across the now dry red wash. Where the layers overlap a coloured grey is created.

Red and green are opposites (complementaries) on the colour circle and when mixed, neutralize each other to make a black or grey.

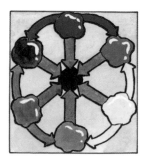

All the complementary mixes do this, but each mix creates a grey with different qualities.

# Surface mixing

### FIRST STAGE

This is an exercise for both wet-on-wet layering and using overlays of complementary colours for mixing. The first stage comprises the first three layers of the image. The base colour used throughout is a bright blue green secondary mix (shown on right). Applied wet-on-wet the contrast between light and darks (value) is developed, which suggests light and depth. A Hake brush is used to wet the surface and a round brush to apply the colour.

Once this layer is dry, it is rewetted overall with the Hake brush and given a complementary layer of red [Rp+ro], the idea being to match the values of the green beneath exactly. To do this with absolute precision is an impossibility and you can see how the surface mixes already become exciting due to their variety and irregularity (shown in middle).

Finally, a yellow layer ([Yo] plus [ro+bp]) is applied and yellow green now becomes dominant (shown on left).

### SECOND STAGE

The final stage is the addition of a complementary mix for the yellow - purple [Bp+rp]. Since the fourth layer has now been reached we are on the very edge of what the watercolour surface can take. To keep surface damage at bay, each section of the painting is now wetted separately with a large round brush. This is allowed to dry thoroughly before the next section is attempted. As the final layer of a layered watercolour is usually the most dominant, the picture now takes on an overall purple bias. Even though the purple is dulled by the other underlying colours, note how exciting the surface remains. Other colours seep through and the yellow, which is the complementary to the purple, becomes the light source in both the sky and the door behind the figures.

# Exercise

**SURFACE COLOUR MIXING WITH WATER**

Three fine tipped medium to small brushes are required for this exercise. The first is used to wet the surface to such an extent that ridges or pools of water are created (right). Paint is dropped into this using a second brush (left). The surface tension of the water pulls the colour along the tube of water. Should this natural percolation of the colour be insufficient, then it can be aided by dropping more water into the pool next to the colour (centre). Colour flow is rapid as a consequence. The third brush is kept to drop in a second colour where necessary.

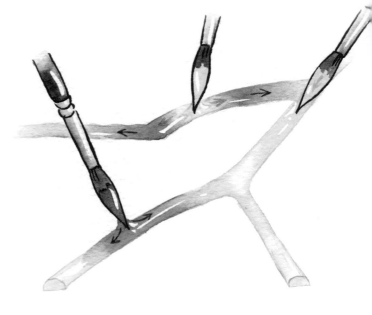

**SURFACE COLOUR MIXING WITH COLOUR**

The majority of the leaf areas are not wetted before painting, but are simply created by first applying the green and then swiftly adding the red before it dries. The two colours flow into and mix with each other naturally. In some cases the red has more water in the mix, sometimes the green and at other times both solutions are equal. The depth of the applied pool of colour can also influence mixing - the fluid naturally flowing from deep deposits in to shallow ones.

*This technique depends* on the use of very restricted wet-into-wet. While the surface around the subject is dry, the branches and leaves are fluid with paint mix.

As with Wet on Dry, the colours dry with a natural hard edge. In fact, a fine wall of pigment is deposited along the colour edge, making it even more powerfully delineated.

On the other hand, the internal colours merge into one another, reflecting the characteristics of painting wet-into-wet. Patience is required, allowing the colours to naturally flow, in order not to overwork the paint.

The colour mix for the branches is a dull green ([Bg+yo] plus [ro]). On the majority of the leaves

the warmer red [Ro+rp+yo] and the warmer green ([Bg+Yg] plus [ro]) are mixed with differing quantities of water.

The secret of success in this type of surface mixing is to learn to apply the colour, and then leave the paint alone. The deep pools of colour, brimming with water, are deceptive and will dry to quite a different appearance than when wet. Not only will the colour dirty if you try to over-control it, but you will stop its natural flow. It is enough to control the silhouette of leaf and twig. Concentrate on their balance and the negative shapes they make (the spaces between the shapes) with pure white paper all around them.

# Common problems

| PROBLEM | ANSWER |
| --- | --- |
| *I am constantly asked the question - 'What colour should I use for white?' or 'What colour is white?'* | The Colours of White and Primary Layering<br>*The truth is that white is actually always a colour. It is influenced by the colours all around it and by the amount of light it receives. So it will always be different. When you look at white you must have something to compare it with so that you can identify its colour. Look around until you can find something else that is white or very light. Now compare it to the original item. How does it differ? Usually you will identify that one is one colour and the other is another by comparison.* |

## *But how do you paint it?*

**SOLUTION**

White is usually a coloured grey. That is, it is a colour, albeit a very dull one, but one that is usually also very light. By overlaying all of the primaries a grey is created. As previously demonstrated, overlaying colours is never perfect and this imperfection is an asset.

*Try painting this egg.*
Start by scuffing on its highlight in masking fluid, picking up the texture of the paper.

**A** - When dry, paint over a layer of thin red [Rp+Ro].
**B** - When thoroughly dry, paint over a layer of thin yellow [Yg+Yo]. Try to match the coverage of the red below as closely as possible.
**C** - Wait until dry before painting over a layer of blue [Bp+Bg], again matching the gradation.

This process creates a coloured grey, which may not look much like white, while it has the white of the paper next to it.

**D** - Apply a dark grey across the background white of the paper - mixed from all the colours you have already used. Remove the masking fluid to expose the highlights and you will now note how the egg now appears white by contrast to the dark background.

Whenever you create a white in such a fashion it will have a bias toward one of the colours. Try to ensure that this bias matches the general colours surrounding the white. Then it will appear that the white of the object is being influenced by its surroundings.

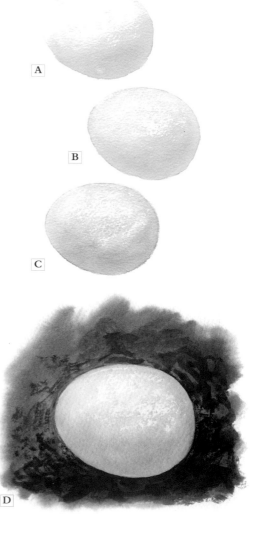

A

B

C

D

# Discovering paint qualities

*To use watercolour effectively you must understand the natural characteristics and capabilities of the paint. Once you do, the potential is enormous.*

*Watercolour is a transparent medium. But what exactly does this mean? The medium referred to is the glue that fixes the colour (pigment) to the surface. In the case of watercolour, this is a gum that dissolves in water. Thus the paint dissolves in water.*

*The solutions of paint and water are known as washes and because there is no opaque or white pigment in the colour, these washes are transparent.*

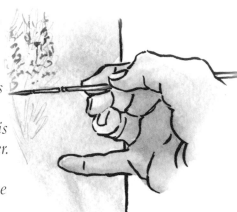

**LIGHT FALLING ON** a wash passes through the paint layer and, bouncing back from the white paper beneath, creates a purity of colour quite different from any other painting medium.

Since the paint dissolves in water, it can be applied to a layer of water already on the paper. This technique, known as Wet on Wet, produces qualities that are again, quite unique to watercolour painting.

Water can be resisted, or prevented from reaching the paper surface. So too can paint. Wax and wax pencils, or crayons, will do the job. There are also special fluid resists that are painted onto the paper and later removed. This allows for the white of the paper to be used as the whites in a painting, rather than having to use opaque whites. Once again, this adds to the richness of the medium.

Because of its transparency, the paint can be applied in layers. Since the medium dissolves in

water, it can be partially or wholly removed, before and after it has dried, offering a new range of transparencies.

The exercise and project that follow, will help you determine how best to exploit these wonderful paints. How many paint layers can be employed without affecting the transparency? What is the difference in mixing paints in layers, as opposed to mixing them on the palette? What is the effect of removing paint and can it be used as a technique in its own right? How should resist be used and where will it be most effective?

The answer to these questions can only be found by trying out the exercise and painting on the following pages. There is no faster way of learning than by taking up your paintbrush and mixing and applying paint. If a wash goes wrong, work out why it happened and try again. You can be relaxed when you remember that it can always be washed off and repainted.

ARTSTRIPS ©

BACKGROUND – very light washes, comprising paint introduced to a puddle of water on the palette.

Let first yellow wash [Yo+ro] plus [bp] dry. Add slightly more pigmented strokes of purple mix ([Rp+Bp] plus [yg]) to suggest gentle shadow.

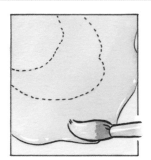

Rewet area beneath each object using large round brush. Go well beyond area to be painted...

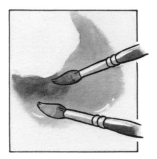

...so that strokes of colour for shadows have soft edges. Start with dull yellow. Add stronger dull purple toward object (mixes as before).

LIME – Protect highlights with masking fluid. Irregular line of mask down sharp cut edge of lime will stop colour flowing beyond.

[FIRST LAYER] Apply light yellow green over whole fruit. While still wet, stroke in yellow green and dark blue green.

[SECOND LAYER] Remove mask. Repaint with yellow green. Stroke in stronger mixes of yellow and dark green. Texture & contrast established.

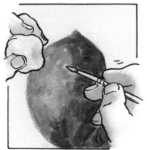

Lift off highlights with wet, small round brush.

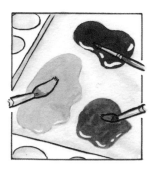

WALNUTS – Prepare three colour mixes on palette, using progressively stiffer mixes for the darker colours.

Lay the lighter colour first. Take care to work right up to the edges.

While still wet, stroke in darker orange to suggest shadow. Use smaller brush to add stiff purple line-work and accents.

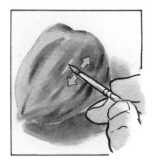

Lift off soft highlights with small round brush.

# Exercise

**THIS EXERCISE IS** all about applying the paint simply and fluidly, in as few layers as possible. Even strong dark colours can remain pure, as long as they are not overworked.

The general rule is not to use more than three layers of dried colour. In other words, at one wetting you may add several colours to an area and several on the next wetting. What causes problems is when a wet layer disturbs the dry layer of paint beneath. Pigments can mix unpleasantly and gum (the glue that holds the paint together) can rise to the surface. You need to avoid the unpleasant staining that results. Keep your paint layers simple and be rewarded with luscious transparent colours.

**MASKING FLUID AND** lift-off are used here to reduce the thickness of paint layers. Masking fluid was applied twice to the lime flesh. Look carefully at the scuffed textures here. You will observe that the extensive masking applied at the beginning of the painting was removed and over-painted. Smaller areas were, however, remasked, hence the tiny highlights of white that remain. As these are the only bits of white paper that are left, you can see they work as white, almost as if white paint had been used.

| COLOUR REFERENCE | COLOUR MIXING |
|---|---|
| Red-purple [Rp]<br>Red-orange [Ro]<br>Blue-purple [Bp]<br>Blue-green [Bg]<br>Yellow-orange [Yo]<br>Yellow-green [Yg] | Where the pre-fix letter is shown in capitals this denotes a larger quantity of that particular colour.<br>   Conversely, where the pre-fix letter is shown in a lower case, this denotes a smaller quantity of that particular colour.<br><br>Example:<br>Bp = **large** amount of blue-purple<br>bp = **small** amount of blue-purple |

The soft crescent curve of the plate contains and holds the eye within the compostion

Masked highlights of white are sharp and focussed

Lifted highlights are soft and textured

# Stage-by-stage

**STAGE 1**

A 0.5 automatic pencil is used to produce a loose and scribbly initial drawing. Try to ascertain the character of the shapes and rhythms of the composition, rather than thinking of it as a tree. Note how the low horizon (distant water level) serves to emphasise the stature and scale of the tree. Use a kneadable putty rubber as you go along, to tighten up the drawing and keep it clean. You can be relatively strong with this drawing, as it will be easily overdrawn with the ink line to follow and then erased. Once completed, switch to a Rigger brush, loaded with black, non-soluble Indian ink to rework. If right-handed, start at the top left of the composition to avoid smudging. If left-handed, start top right. Draw in the silhouette of leaf and branch. The purpose is not to merely reinforce the pencil line, but to use it as a rough guide. Attempt to discover the character of line that will reflect the structure of the tree growth. This descriptive line should be fluid and move freely, guided but not restricted by the pencil work beneath. When dry, use the putty rubber to gently erase any remaining pencil lines.

*Finally* – with a small round brush apply masking fluid to protect berries, branch highlights and blades of grass at the base.

> **Kneadable putty rubber** - As its name implies, this is a flexible malleable rubber.
> Ideal for gently rubbing away, reducing or dabbing off unwanted pencil lines. Most importantly, without damaging the surface of the paper.

Both the pencil and ink line-work needs to be loose and fluid. By supporting your hand you will gain more confidence to do this. The simple trick is to extend your small finger and allow it to touch the surface of the paper – this provides the necessary support, while not restricting the movement of the other fingers as they sweep the pencil or brush across the surface. Think of this as your hand skating across the paper as would a skater across ice and you will get the feel of this technique. As a bonus, when applying the pencil line, it prevents too much pressure being applied to the paper, which could damage its surface.

When using the Rigger loaded with ink – starting at the top of the composition means you are less likely to smear the ink with your finger as you work down.

## STAGE 2

**THE OBJECT OF THIS** study is to apply and remove the paint layers as simply as possible, regardless of the strength or darkness of the mix. In this way, the transparency of the watercolours can be fully exploited and explored. Since all of the drawing of the subject is conveyed by the ink line, you can concentrate on enjoying the paint application in its own right. Thus you will observe and learn how the control of the thickness of the paint layer is essential in ensuring that the rich luminescent character of the paint is retained.

**WET ON WET** - First, wet the whole surface with any large brush and with a large round brush, apply thin colour to sky, distant hill and leaves. Heavier colour is needed for the water and foreground grass.

**WET ON DRY** –Using round brushes, revisit the hill and leaves, creating textures and accents. The colour along tree limbs are applied so swiftly that they run into one another. Greens are then given contrast, by having a purple shadow worked over them, losing its edges to give the limbs volume. When dry, the masking fluid is removed with the putty rubber.

**THE TREE LIMB** shadows require edges to be lost in two directions. On the left, the still wet purple wash down the right side of the trunk is lost by laying water down its left edge. The result is seen to the right – a graded wash suggesting the roundness of the branch. Alternatively, the wash could be lost, top and bottom, to different effect. Both of these effects could be applied to a single branch. The pools of water and paint on the diagrams have been made to look deep in order to suggest their wetness. However, you must experiment with each, discovering by doing so just how deep each area needs to be laid to achieve the desired result.

MASKING FLUID REMOVED

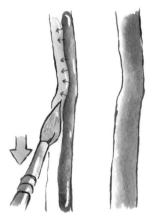

BUILDING TREE LIMB SHADOWS

⇧ **Always keep in** your mind that fluidity is more important than accuracy, to keep the line-work exciting. This is a painting, not a photograph and the character of the surface makes all the difference.

⇦ **Note** how the combination of masking and lifting off creates both volume and texture. See how soft edges to shadow suggest rounded form, while sharp edges indicate shadow cast by other limbs.

⇨ **The transparent red** of the berries glows out as a complementary contrast to the dark green of the foliage. While the berries are placed as irregularly as possible, you will note that these make up a rhythm of shapes that carry our eye, as they ripple across the surface.

## STAGE 3

Upon removing the masking fluid from berries, tree limbs and blades of grass, gaps in the paint layer appear, through which the white of the paper is revealed. All of the edges of these areas are sharp, since that is the nature of masking fluid. In this stage some of these edges are softened and the colour around them is thinned, by lifting the paint.

First, the berries are all painted with a small brush. Once dry, some are rewet with a small round brush and dabbed lighter with an absorbent tissue.

A flat nylon brush is used to remove colour around the masked areas on the trunks, giving them a softer, rounded profile.

The sky needs a softer approach and is softened with a wet Hake, before gently lifting off. Discover the different effects achieved by dabbing or smearing as you lift the colour with an absorbent tissue.

Heavy layers of paint, such as those on the water, ground and rocks are lifted very gradually. Wetting, dabbing, wetting, dabbing, again and again, until the required degree of transparency has been achieved. If these areas become too chalky, they can be corrected by applying broad strokes of thin light colour.

Once the colour has been successfully completed the whole painting can be revisited with the Rigger and more line added, completing the drawing and creating accents and texture. Wherever the line becomes too heavy, immediately dab gently with a tissue, while still wet, to lighten.

# Common problems

**PROBLEM**

*Lift-off should be easy, but if you are not aware of one particular and very simple problem, it can lead to failure and the deepest frustration. This problem is not uncommon, neither is it exclusive to someone new to painting.*

**CAUSE AND RESULT**

*The answer lies in the paper and it is something that cannot be seen on the surface, only experienced while painting. Attempts to lift-off result in something that is feint at best, non-existent at worst.*

## Solution

The solution is simple and the problem can be avoided through understanding about paper and its reaction to the paint.

**Fig. 1** - Paper is made from fibres that are held together with glue. This glue is known as size and this size inside the paper is referred to as 'internal size'. Watercolour paper has a layer of size on its surface – referred to as the 'external size'. When dry, this external size forms a strong layer, which protects the paper during drawing and erasing. The difficulty being that some papers have less size than others.

**Figs. 2 & 3** - If a paper is well sized it will be less absorbent. On the other hand if it is not well sized, it will become absorbent. The more absorbent the paper the faster it will dry and the deeper the colour will penetrate.

**Fig. 4** - When watercolour paper is painted, the paint can come to rest in three layers. The size layer softens with the water and most of the pigment becomes fixed within. Strong colours may penetrate more deeply and they can stain the fibres. Heavy paint layers are sometimes left on the surface above the size.

**Fig. 5** - Layers of paint on the surface are the most vulnerable. These can float away when the surface is rewet.

**Fig. 6** - However, paint held by the now jelly-like size will not move until it is disturbed by the friction of a brush – this is how lift-off works.

**Fig. 7** - On the other hand, fibres that have absorbed pigment will not release the stain, unless they themselves are removed.

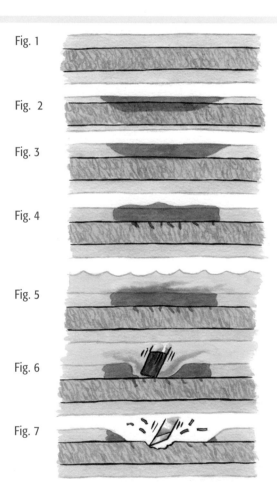

Fig. 1

Fig. 2

Fig. 3

Fig. 4

Fig. 5

Fig. 6

Fig. 7

*It is important* therefore to experiment with paint and papers until you find a combination that lifts–off to your satisfaction. Papers that are absorbent often produce wonderful textures as the fibres absorb the pigment, but it is less easy to make changes. Only you can decide which is preferable.

# Exploiting brush-strokes

*Just as many find making the first pencil marks on a piece of white paper one of the hardest things to do, it can also prove quite intimidating to pick up a paintbrush and create the first strokes of a painting. Yet, as soon as you do so, you will have broken through that barrier.*

*Let me assure you that everyone feels that sense of insecurity at the start. The brush is a fine instrument, through which you will communicate and share your ideas, abilities and creativity with others.*

*However, the inherent qualities in this piece of equipment need to be learnt and how to harness them. The process will always involve making mistakes along the way, so do go easy on yourself.*

**YOU HAVE ALREADY** learned about some of the basic shapes and are now familiar with how each can be used. Now give yourself time to become acclimatised to the feel of each of them in your hand. Eventually they will become an extension of your hand – getting to know them so well that you will 'hear' when they are wet or dry, 'feel' whether they are the right size and shape for the job.

The Samurai of Japan were taught to 'love the paint brush' as much as the sword and you too will gain as much from them, if you are prepared to make the effort.

In the following pages we explore the differences between the various brushes. What happens when they are drawn across both wet and dry surfaces;

what results when the angle of the brush to the paper surface is altered? A seemingly simple question – what is the difference between using a large or a small brush when drawing detail?

The unknowing might answer a small brush is better. Yet, a large brush could offer just as small a point, while holding more paint and thus go further before the need to reload. Experience will teach you much, but it is far better to venture forth with a good guide to the basics.

The Artstrips that follow demonstrate how to successfully accomplish the accompanying exercise on reflection. Keep trying this exercise until you feel confident to move on to the following stage-by-stage painting.

ARTSTRIPS©

SMALL ROUND BRUSH
- apply masking fluid. Draw
across paper at a shallow
angle.

LARGE ROUND BRUSH - [SKY]
apply fluid graduated wash.
Scuff at tree edges by holding
at a shallow angle as it runs
out of paint.

[TREES] use same brush to
apply fluid washes. Block in
trees as solid masses. Keep
brush on paper surface.

MEDIUM ROUND BRUSH
- loaded with stiffer paint. Pull
in various directions to create
inner structure and shadows
of trees.

HAKE BRUSH - [bottom half of
painting] wet surface swiftly.
Keep board upright so excess
water runs off and does not
pool.

LARGE ROUND BRUSH -
[bottom half of painting] brush
loaded and shaped with stiff
colour. Pull along waterline
beneath trees.

Reload same brush and pull
vertically. Ease pressure toward
bottom of stroke so that colour
fades.

HAKE BRUSH - rewet when
area is dry. MEDIUM ROUND
BRUSH - loaded with stiffer
paint. Apply horizontal wave
paterns.

When dry, remove mask-
ing fluid. FLAT BRUSH - wet.
Soften paint inside flowers and
on waves beneath. Lift off with
absorbent tissue.

HAKE BRUSH - rewet same
areas. SMALL ROUND BRUSH
- drop in colour.

MEDIUM ROUND BRUSH -
lightly loaded. Hold flat against
surface and scuff on dry colour
to lily pads.

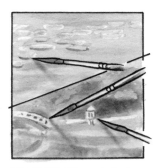

RIGGER BRUSH - apply final
line detail to base of lilies. Also
bridge and bank - focal points.

# Exercise

**THIS EXERCISE IS** designed to use all of the brushes to which you have been introduced. To experience first hand the sort of strokes they make and the qualities inherent in each.

Every brush–stroke used here will be used again in the stage-by-stage painting to follow. In this study however, they are not so intricately woven into or over each other. Simple layers mean that you can see individual strokes wet. Watch changes as they dry and retain a record for future reference.

The top half of the painting is painted almost entirely using the Wet on Dry technique, with the exception of the crimson coloration of the flowers. Pan colours are used here so that you can experience brush mixing, brush loading and application from the pan palette.

As a result the top half of the painting consists of shapes with relatively sharp edges, a natural consequence of painting wet-on-dry.

In contrast, the bottom half of the painting is painted mostly with the Wet on Wet technique, with the exception of the lilies, which contrast strongly against the soft blur of colours that surround them.

Tube colours are worked with in the wet-on-wet areas to provide the stiff, dark, paint mixes required for this technique.

The subject is purely imaginative, designed to give the qualities of brush-stroke necessary for your development at this stage.

## NOTE

THE IMPORTANCE OF THE YELLOW GREENS USED IN THE PAINTING. THESE ARE IMPORTANT, FOR WITHOUT THEM THERE WOULD BE AN ABSENCE OF SUNLIGHT.

Sharp wet-on-dry edges can remain distant and gently focused, provided that the value contrast at their edge is kept minimal

Brushstrokes into the wet interior of the tree are soft-edged and gently focussed, despite strong value contrast

Strong contrast, along with the sharp edges of the lilies, attract the eye, creating maximum focus

# Stage-by-stage

The simplicity of a boat and its reflection is a subject of universal appeal. However, simplicity hides subtle angles and suggestions in the composition, which must be recognized, if the painting is to work. Note for example how the line of the boat (direction in which it is pointing) is picked up by the weed on the water. Together they seem to move to the left and up, as if toward some distant point. This echoes a vanishing point of perspective and gives the image depth. You will also discover that the dry land, which forms a steep triangle bottom right, curves up and out, cradling the subject. The same is true for the reflection and shadow of the boat.

## STAGE 1

As this is a Wet on Dry painting, in which the hard-edged washes will cover easily, the drawing can be applied relatively strongly. Allow the pencil work around rocks and weed to become more erratic. It is a waste of time recording every detail, but it is important to feel the general mass and movement within these areas. Masking fluid is exploited here to protect fine highlights and the ripples in the water. It also masks areas where subsequently applied colours need to be kept clean and translucent. When using the masking fluid, keep strokes as varied as those used to apply paint, as their direction and size will also help to establish the rhythms of the subject.

TIP: Draw the rope lines as a single pencil line. The masking fluid applied over the line will make the rope naturally thicker.

*Getting the boat correct.* Boats are composed of a series of subtle curves that can feel difficult to reproduce. Make things simpler for yourself – reduce them first to a series of straight, but angled, lines.

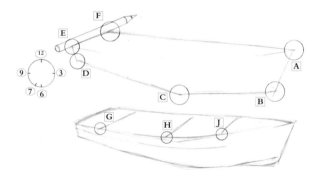

### WORKING OUT ANGLES

1. Hold your pencil length against any line to determine the angle of that line.
2. Visualise your pencil length as being the hour hand on a clock-face.
3. To which position does the angle at which your pencil now lies correspond on the clock-face?
4. Is it at 12 o'clock, 3 o'clock, 6 o'clock, 9 o'clock - or somewhere in between, such as 7 o'clock?

*Look at the boat in this painting, corresponding to the diagram.*

**A.** The angles are at 10 o'clock, 8 o'clock and 7 o'clock.
**E & F.** The pencil moves through both faces at 2 o'clock.
**B, C & D.** Where do these lie?

Once you have determined these angles, they can be gently turned into curves. Look for further angles such as **G, H & J** to add further details.

## STAGE 2

### HAKE BRUSH AND LARGE ROUND BRUSH

The water is painted first. Use a Hake brush to wet the whole area so that brush-strokes will be soft. Load a large round brush with thin colour (not too heavily). Create downward strokes to mimic the reflections. Then, with a slightly stiffer colour, the same large round brush is used to weave patterns of horizontal and slightly angular strokes.

### LARGE ROUND BRUSH - *Head and Point Technique*

For the yellow of the boats reflection, a much stiffer mix is applied, using the whole side of the head of the large round brush. While still wet, the point of the same brush creates the fine green detail of rock and weed. The same head and point technique is employed for the stones, using a warm orange wash, followed by scribbled wet-in-wet detail.

### LARGE & SMALL ROUND BRUSHES

Painting the boat is quite different. While round brushes are used, the paint is taken from a pan palette (refer to Exercise). All paint is applied wet-on-dry. In large areas - washes are laid and then, while still wet, others are introduced (restricted wet-on-wet). Small detailed areas are painted with smaller brushes, their colours being changed as the wash progresses. When dry, the masking fluid is removed.

**THE CONCEPT OF** working colour into wet washes does involve timing, so you may feel it sensible to pre-mix the colours involved, before you lay the first brush-stroke. For the area on the left - use the shoulder of the large round brush to wash over a dull yellow mix. Note how in the centre another colour (red) has been introduced, again using the shoulder of the brush. The pressure applied and stiffness of the mix will affect the strength of the resultant stroke. To the right - use the point of the brush, or perhaps a smaller brush, to produce line, rather than stroke. Since this is being painted into the wet wash, it will be softy focussed. If you are speedy, both elements could be applied to the same area.

MASKING FLUID IN PLACE

MASKING FLUID REMOVED

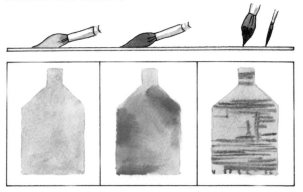

WORKING COLOUR INTO WET WASH

## STAGE 3

Generally, all the washes on the boat and the beach are now accomplished wet-on-dry, using pan colours. However, the small amount of reworking on the water still needs to be done wet-in-wet using the Hake brush. This brush really comes into its own now, as you can rewet the painted surface without lifting already laid colour.

Smaller round brushes and Rigger brushes are used side-on, to produce warm scuffs and scumbles over weed and stone. Their points are used for line-work and drawing, wherever sharp focus is required.

Areas of colour, such as the boat shadow and weed beds on the shore, are given a broad wash of colour and then worked over – both whilst wet and when dry – scumbling texture and losing edges, to provide as much variety to the surface as possible. In the water, some soft horizontal highlights are lifted off with a small, flat nylon brush.

## COLOUR NOTE

*We read the boat as being white. yet, the only white is the highlight on the inside. move your eye from this spot back and forth between all the other 'white' areas and you will see the 'coloured greys' involved.*

⇧ **Although several wettings** are required in which to apply all of the colour for the water, the resultant softness is the perfect foil for the hard-edged strokes of the land and boat. Water takes up over half of the painted surface and yet our eyes fix mainly on brush-strokes with sharp edges.

⇧ **The difference between** wet and dry stones and weed are created by painting either wet-on-wet or wet-on-dry. Note how the details beneath the water have duller highlights and lighter accents.

⇦ **Horizontal bands along** the boat are a wonderful example of how rapid colour change enabled by the use of pan colours and a small brush can produce exciting colour in the details.

### Small Brush-Strokes

Wet on Dry brush-strokes are applied to rocks above and beneath water using a small round brush and a Rigger.

### Medium Brush-Strokes

Wet on Dry graded colours are applied over the boat using a medium round brush. Most of these colours are mixed in the brush head.

### Large Brush-Strokes

Wet on Wet horizontal and vertical strokes on the water are complemented with further layers, using the Hake and the large round brush.

Note the perspective in these strokes, as they gently graduate toward a vanishing point up and out of the painting to the right. This adds further depth to the composition as a whole.

# Common problems

## LOSING EDGES

Let us look at the right and wrong way to lose edges and why the technique can go awry. Understanding precisely what is happening will put you back in control.

**Green Brush-Strokes.** *Left illustration* - note how this stroke has hard edges. We need to soften the right hand edge of that stroke with a wet brush.

*Middle illustration* - this shows that if the wet brush-stroke is overlaid too widely with water, the paint becomes disturbed to a far grater degree than we need. Too much water can even cause a back-run, as the water flowing into the colour carries a wall of pigment ahead of it, creating the characteristic 'cauliflower' effect.

*Right illustration* - the correct way to soften an edge. Instead of the water being laid over the brush-stroke, it is laid alongside. The colour will then naturally flow into it - therefore losing the edge.

**Orange Brush-Strokes.** *Left illustration* - as before, the stroke has hard edges.

*Middle illustration* - the second stroke again overlaps the first. This time however, the brush is not just loaded with water, but with a more dilute colour of the original stroke. Now the pigment and gum contained in the second stroke make it more compatible with the first and a graded colour results.

*Right illustration* - the edge of the brush-stroke is lost by lying a stroke of water alongside.

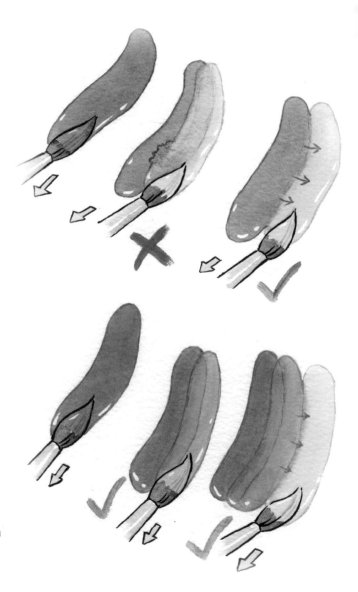

# Exploiting palette mixing

*Using your palette efficiently comes into its own when painting flowers. We are all dazzled by the colours of flowers and their form and, of course, they make the perfect subject for any artist, no matter what the painter's level of skill.*

*Most of us have access to flowers, whether live or as photographs. For those new to painting, they offer a perfect opportunity for honing skills in mixing and delivering paint to the paper's surface; their secret being the purity of colour required.*

**LOOK INTO THE** deepest shadows of a flower head and you will find a luscious intensity of colour. We have already discovered that to create really dark colours, you need to mix in complementaries. Complementary colours, however, also dull colour mixes down.

With a flower petal, the trick is to keep the use of complementary colours to a minimum and rely instead, on tonal change, through controlling the density of pigment. In other words, to make a colour dark in this instance, you simply use more of the same colour.

Once mixed, the colour must be transferred from the palette in a way that will create a smooth, even layer of paint that will mimic the soft qualities of the petals. Thus the palette must be fully utilised, from mixing the colour efficiently and controlling the amount of paint employed, to the delivery of the colour to the painting itself.

There is much to be discovered and at your own pace. Now you can begin to use your palette as a wonderful tool with which to achieve the spectrum of colours needed for future paintings.

How should your palette be used for graded washes?

How do layered washes differ in quality and mix on the palette surface?

When can complementaries be added?

What is the difference between mixing complementaries on the palette and adding them directly to the painting?

The following Artstrips, exercise and project are designed to acquaint you with other options at your disposal when using your palette.

BACKGROUND - *Large fluid mix on palette of colour plus water*. Mix well in brush head as well as in main body of fluid.

More water added throughout the wash. Ensure thorough mixing of whole solution at each stage.
Applied wet-on-dry.

SHADOW UNDER APPLES - Mix as before but with less water and add [Bp].

Pull brush across palette surface to remove excess colour from brush, before applying wet-on-wet.

DISTANT FRUIT - *Small mix on palette, graduated colour*. Mix small quantity of green [Bg+Yg] using medium round brush. Apply wet-on-dry.

Now introduce red to edge of mix, pulling in some of the green mix. Apply wet-on-dry before previous colour dries on the paper.

Continue adding red to edge of previous mix to control graduation of colour change.

TOP OF FRUIT - Add water alone to mix edge to lighten.

RED FRUIT - *Brush-head mix on palette*. Dampen brush. Load with colour. Transfer to palette and use surface to evenly mix colour within brush head.

VALUE CHANGE - Lay colour and return brush to water jar. Dip head into water - do not shake. Return brush to palette and mix in brush head as before.

As fruit lightens, repeat process, Find new spot on palette for each mix.

To lighten green on leaves. Use same technique with smaller brush.

# Exercise

Within this simple exercise you will find all the variety of palette mixes and subsequent methods of application that you will need to use in the more detailed flower painting which follows. If one of the areas begins to go wrong for you, simply wash over swiftly, before it dries, using a big brush heavily loaded with water. Lift the paint off with an absorbent tissue, allow to dry, and then have another go.

| COLOUR REFERENCE | COLOUR MIXING |
|---|---|
| Red-purple [Rp]<br>Red-orange [Ro]<br>Blue-purple [Bp]<br>Blue-green [Bg]<br>Yellow-orange [Yo]<br>Yellow-green [Yg] | Where the pre-fix letter is shown in capitals this denotes a larger quantity of that particular colour.<br><br>Conversely, where the pre-fix letter is shown in a lower case, this denotes a smaller quantity of that particular colour.<br><br>Example:<br>Bp = **large** amount of blue-purple<br>bp = **small** amount of blue-purple |

**GENTLY DRAW IN** the shapes, using a 0.5 automatic pencil. Add the washes, remembering to keep your brush on the surface as much as possible, so that they flow evenly. If there is any pooling of colour, lift these off with a squeezed 'thirsty' brush to prevent back-runs forming.

Most of the colours are to be applied onto a dry surface, except the closest red fruit. For this, the surface is wetted with a large round brush, before the colour is applied.

Similarly, the area beneath the fruit is wetted first, so that the shadow edges can be soft when applied. In the wetting of this section, you will need to do so well beyond the intended shadow edges, to ensure a successful outcome.

Edges lost with water appear along the top of the brushstrokes, which indicate the dimples on the top of the fruit. You will need to have a second wet brush ready to do the job swiftly when you try this.

Also note that the colour of the leaf at the rear is created by mixing red [Ro] plus green [Bg+Yg] on the palette. For the front leaf, the green is painted first, then, when dry, a thin red is overlaid (layering).

## NOTE

Every time you do this exercise the result will inevitably be slightly different. Do not let this worry you. Instead, learn from the natural qualities inherent in the paint as it dries.

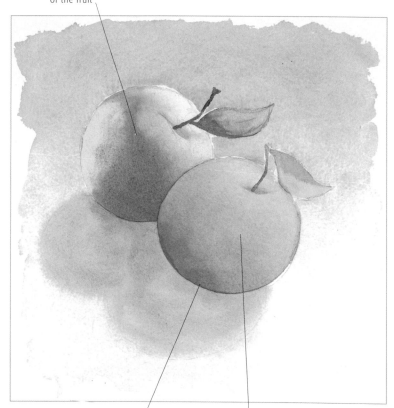

Colour changes as progressive wet-on-dry strokes are lost into one another across the surface of the fruit

Edges of wash dry hard to produce a focussed silhouette

Colour changes as progressive wet-on-wet strokes run into each other across the skin of the fruit

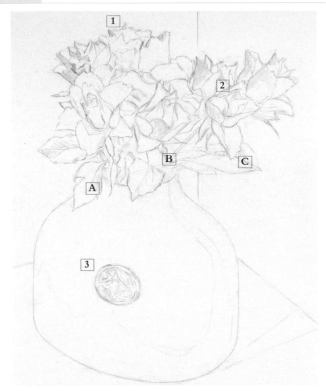

# Stage-by-stage

### STAGE 1

The composition is gently drawn in with a 0.5 automatic pencil, and then overlaid with masking fluid applied with a small/medium round, sable brush. In this painting the masking fluid is employed to serve several functions.

1. Along the top edges of petals it will sharply separate them from the strong background colour to be subsequently applied.

2. Elsewhere on the flower heads it is used to hold back the flow of colour from one petal to its neighbour.

3. It creates texture by being scuffed, just like paint, over the paper surface (note the medallion on the vase).

| COLOUR REFERENCE | | COLOUR MIXING |
|---|---|---|
| | | Where the pre-fix letter is shown in capitals this denotes a larger quantity of that particular colour. |
| Red-purple | [Rp] | |
| Red-orange | [Ro] | |
| Blue-purple | [Bp] | Conversely, where the pre-fix letter is shown in a lower case, this denotes a smaller quantity of that particular colour. |
| Blue-green | [Bg] | |
| Yellow-orange | [Yo] | |
| Yellow-green | [Yg] | |
| | | Example: |
| | | Bp = **large** amount of blue-purple |
| | | bp = **small** amount of blue-purple |

**WHEN DRAWING FLOWERS**, the complexity of their flouncy ebullient petals can be disheartening. Take your time to look below the surface at their underlying structure and simplicity. The first thing that will help is to establish that many flower heads are symmetrical in shape.

Rotate a pencil or an imaginary line through one flower head [A], until you discover the angle which roughly cuts it into two equal halves. You now have the main thrust of the flower shape

Box the general outline of the flower around this line of symmetry [B] and now all those wayward petals can be controlled within that main mass [C]

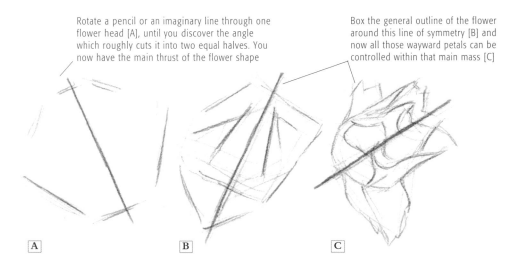

A          B          C

## STAGE 2

### BACKGROUND

At first, the painting is kept flat, to apply the large fluid palette mixes of rich red. On the left hand side these move through secondary mixes from Yellow-orange to almost Red-purple - [Yo] > [Ro] > [Rp]. On the right, the red has its complementary green added to make it graduate to duller and darker intensities and values.

### VASE

Now the painting is placed upright. The greens for the complementary underpainting layer on the vase are mixed much more stiffly on the palette and the paper is wetted with a large round brush before applying the colour. As such, the blending values needed for the soft rounded form of the vase are achieved wet-in-wet using graduated mixes of green – [Yg+Bg]->[Yo+Bg]>[Yo+Bp]. The medallion on the vase is painted yellow [Yg] and while wet, has orange applied [Yg+Ro+bp], to evoke the pattern.

### SHELF

Below the vase is a shelf, the colour for which is a brush-head mix with water that is added to achieve the graduation towards a lighter value on the left hand side.

### LEAVES

These are first washed with a yellow green to wet the surface. Then, while still wet, Blue-green mid-values are stroked on.

### FLOWERS

Again, laid wet-in-wet, these are kept as bright as possible, even in their shadows. Dark colours are mainly achieved through having less water in their mix. However, judicious use of a little purple can result in the introduction of subtle density, without destroying the overall yellow intensity.

   The vase mix on the palette should be stiff enough to shape the brush into a flat chisel shape and the colour changes should be made at the edge of the previous mix for more control. If you mix the whole amount, you will either end up with too much quantity of paint mixed, or the changes will not be dramatic enough.

MASKING FLUID IN PLACE

MASKING FLUID REMOVED

## STAGE 3

### VASE

Three densities of Red-orange fluid mixes, ([Ro] plus [yo+bp]) - light, medium and strong - are premixed on the flat area of the palette. These will provide a layer of red to overpaint the previously applied green. The red needs to be overpainted wet-on-dry, since rewetting the vase would soften the dry green layer. As the red is laid across the vase, water can be added at the side of each wash on the palette, to give an infinite variety of strengths. Should the colours dry a little too light; a second layer of red can be applied, once the first has dried. Edges of this second layer are lost with a wet brush to retain the internal softness of the coloured areas within the vase. For the shadow on the shelf, a yellow with purple ([Yg] plus [ro+bp]), graduated with water, is painted wet-on-dry (brush-head mix). However, its leading edge is lost. The medallion is given a wash of yellow [Yg], lost toward the highlights.

### LEAVES

A yellow-orange wash can be applied to small enough areas for it not to disturb the underlying green, before a brushy, stiffer, application of red purple is added to enrich their accents. Once dry, the 'greenness' of these accents can be reaffirmed if necessary, by overlays of warm or cool green.

### FLOWERS

Glazes of Red-orange are now swept onto the flowers. This is achieved with three brushes. The first is used to stroke on large areas of yellow wash; into which are laid red strokes with a second brush, that define the edge or direction of a petal. The third, small brush, hits the petal edge, just before it dries, to create the sharp red definition.

## NOTE

OBSERVE HOW ON THE LAYERED COLOURS OF VASE AND LEAF IT IS THE FINAL LAYER THAT BECOMES THE DOMINANT OR 'LOCAL' COLOUR.

⇧ **The subtlety of** the layered mixes on the vase provides strong contrast against the simply laid colour of the background. Lifting some red from the wall also helps.

⇧ **Contrast the pure** laid premixed hues of the background red-orange with the glazes of red over the dry yellow on the petals.

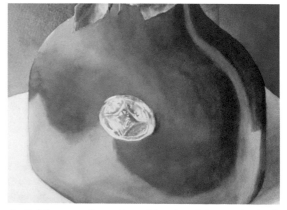

⇧ **Soft focus on** the wet-in-wet layering of the vase body - but the masking of the medallion is sharp and draws our eye.

# Common problems

**PROBLEM**

*Problems may occur when overlaying dark areas of paint. Colours may accidentally lift, simply not be strong enough, or even have become patchy.*

**ANSWER**

*Adding washes to such small areas is simply not practical and in fact can lead to unwanted lift of more of the dark colours. What is required is a way to invisibly mend the patch or the unevenness by 'weaving' pigment into the already dense surface.*

*This can be seen around the dark shadow areas at the top right edge of the vase, where not only was there a little unevenness, but it did become difficult to provide a red wash strong enough to overpower the green.*

**SOLUTION**

Employ soft scuffs of 'dry' colour which can be 'woven' into the existing paint.

**METHOD**

**Fig. 1**
Mix the colour on the palette. No matter whether it is fluid or very stiff, the majority of the paint mix must be eliminated from the brush. To do this, pull the brush head across the clean palette surface, relieving it of excess paint.

**Fig. 2**
The brush head is now flattened as a result of drawing it across the palette. Hold it level with the paper surface, so that it catches the paper texture easily. The gum already present in the dry paint will help to 'pull' the pigment from your brush, so hardly any pressure is required to achieve the desired application.

**Fig. 3**
Gently overlay the scuffs using a hatching motion. Continue until you have achieved the required density of value and/or colour.

This soft texture has no hard edges and is therefore compatible with underlying paint, whether it has been laid wet-in-wet or wet-on-dry.

# Discovering surface texture

*Never underestimate the importance of selecting the right surface on which to work. As with paints, palette and brushes, it is one of the most important tools at an artists disposal.*

*Because we have become familiar with paper throughout our lives, we find it difficult to look beyond the conventional. Why should one type of paper be more expensive than another? Could we not simply paint on everyday paper, such as cartridge paper?*

**IT IS HELPFUL TO FORGET** that the surface on which you are going to paint is paper. It is reasonable to assume that specialist paint requires a surface which works best with that medium. After all, were you to take up oil painting, the surface on which to paint would have to accept the unique properties of oil paints.

Cartridge paper, for instance, is seldom thick enough, nor is it likely to be sized and will therefore be very absorbent. Once paint is applied, it will cockle immediately. Neither will the paper stay wet long enough, which would make it impossible to apply more than one layer of paint. Usually, when the paper does not work, new painters blame it on their lack of skill and often disillusionment sets in. Which is such a shame, especially as the problem can be avoided from the start.

Not only will a good paper have all the qualities to help you achieve good results, it will also last. '*Does longevity matter?*' you may well respond.

At first it will not. However, once you are rewarded by achieving a painting that you wish to keep, then it would be disappointing to find the painting deteriorating over time. It goes without

saying, that any painting being considered for sale should be produced on a non-perishable surface.

Whilst the ideal surface is an artists' quality watercolour paper, there are students' quality versions, which mimic the qualities of their more expensive cousins. The difference being that the cheaper papers are generally made from cellulose (wood) fibres and have been treated to be acid-free, so that they will not yellow rapidly. As you gain in confidence, you will eventually want to move on to the more expensive cotton based papers, which should last a few lifetimes.

There are many different papers available from which to make a choice. The following pages are an introduction to how some surfaces function, but it is important to keep experimenting. As you will settle on a favourite brush, so too will you find a paper that best suits your style.

One of the easiest methods to explore the surface of a paper is by exposing its texture. This section is full of scuffs and scumbles, the best way in which to demonstrate this point and for you to explore the nature of surface textures.

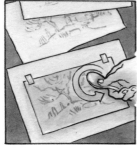

DRAW IDENTICAL IMAGE ON THREE DIFFERENT TEXTURES OF PAPER - produce master drawing on tracing paper. Rub down onto each sheet.

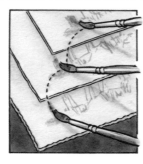

PAINT IDENTICAL IMAGE ON EACH SHEET - for each master stroke on one sheet, repeat identical stroke on other two sheets and compare.

Mix good quantity of stiff dark colour on palette. Take some of this to produce a separate fluid mix.

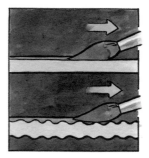

Fluid Colour (light areas) Fluid colour loaded heavily into brush will flow evenly onto the surface, whether surface is textured or not.

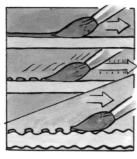

Colour from sparsely loaded brush will not run into textures (bottom) - but to create texture on smooth paper, brush-stroke needs to be speeded up (top).

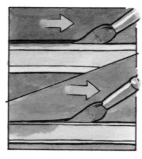

Paper size on surface can also affect the result. Less sized = more absorbency = less easy to avoid solid coverage.

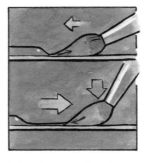

To load brush less heavily, approach pool edge with brush tip and pull colour across palette.

Test on scrap piece of paper before committing to the painting.

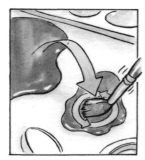

Progressively darken mix. Throughout exercise ensure darkened wash is thoroughly mixed on palette and in brush head.

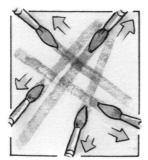

Scuffs are directional. Point brush shaft in direction of the stroke to keep brush head shaped.

Three types of stiff line-work using... (TOP) Corner of flattened point of medium round brush. (MIDDLE) Small round brush. (BOTTOM) Rigger brush.

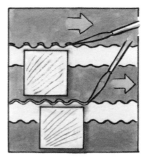

The steeper the angle of a brush, the more likely it is to fill in deeper surface depressions (i.e. Rough paper) and lose texture.

# Exercise

This exercise requires three sheets of watercolour paper of the same weight, but featuring differing degrees of texture, so that a comparison can be made of the resultant effects from painting the same study in exactly the same way.

Hot Pressed [HP]

Not (cold pressed) [CP]

Rough [R]

Keep the paint application simple, with as few layers as possible, in order that you can easily analyse the results of the different marks you are going to make.

Start with the lightest colours in the sky, progressing slowly to the darker washes. Use the same medium round brush for all the scuffs and scumbles, only changing to a Rigger brush for the really dark line-work at the end.

You will first notice how difficult it is to create texture on the smooth paper, using the fluid colour. Speed up the strokes and you will find this helps, as will keeping the brush shaft low to the paper. Note how, as the colour becomes stiffer, there is an increasing variation between the way each surface accepts the paint. Although it will seem natural to compensate for this by increasing the angle of the brush to the surface, to get the paint to stick, this should be avoided, if at all possible, as it will affect the comparison between the surfaces.

Finally, as the line-work is added, you will note that it is the Hot Pressed paper on which this will show more cleanly.

This exercise will help you make an informed decision as to whether you prefer the detailing achieved on the Hot Pressed paper, or the texture afforded by choosing a Rough paper. You will also have a better understanding of the foibles inherent in different papers and compensate for these.

# Stage-by-stage

## STAGE 1

While the texture of the field cannot be fully rendered in pencil, use the underlying drawing (produced with a 0.5 automatic pencil) to identify its rhythms and structures. With such a large area dedicated to the texture of the yellow blossoms, it naturally becomes the main subject of the painting. As such, it is an area that needs focus. Masking fluid is the perfect medium with which to explore the possibilities of sharp texture, which the NOT paper surface has to offer. As in the application of paint, the masked strokes are guided, but not restricted, by the drawing beneath. They are directional, using different brushes to exploit the surface in a variety of ways.

At the top of the field, use small round brushes to produce the small strokes, suggesting distance. These become larger in brush and stroke size the lower you move, as the subject becomes progressively closer. In the foreground switch to a Rigger brush to catch the paper with linear strokes, pulled upward.

Brush shoulders are employed, dabbing as well as dragging (scuffing). A dab can be thought of as a static scuff and leaves a quite different impression on the NOT paper.

## NOTE

ON OTHER PAPERS THESE EFFECTS WOULD ALL BE QUITE DIFFERENT.

### PREPARING A BRUSH TO USE WITH MASKING FLUID

It is crucial to slow down the drying of masking fluid in the brush head to avoid damaging it.

**1.** Wet the brush head.
**2.** Flick off excess water and transfer the head to a bar of soap [A] or dip into household liquid soap [B].
**3.** Work soap into the brush hairs with your fingers, ensuring it is thoroughly coated inside and out [C].
**4.** Wipe off excess soap with an absorbent tissue [D] before loading with masking fluid.

The soap slows down the drying of the masking fluid and helps to work it free when the brush is cleaned in water. This process may need to be repeated several times if large areas of mask are to be applied.

## STAGE 2

Premix a grey for the sky that will really contrast and throw out the yellow field below. Wet the sky, not with water alone, but with a band of colour washes. These start the left as blue, move to the centre as red and are completed on the right as yellow. While still wet, the grey is painted into them wet-on-wet. This has the effect of varying the colour of the grey, making it less neutral and thus more exciting to the eye.

The yellows of the field should be painted swiftly, wet-on-dry - the textures of the surface are exposed as the colour is rejected from the masked scuffs. The lower greens are painted wet-on-wet, so that they can be made soft and dark in areas. Once again the masks show through. When the masking fluid is removed it is immediately apparent that the masking does not appear as extensive when colour is present. This is always the case and you must bear it in mind when applying the mask, so that you do not underestimate the amount required.

## REMOVING DRIED MASK FROM THE SURFACE

Before attempting to remove the mask, ensure that the surface is completely dry. Paper can tear and, or, paint can smear if it is not so. Test this by gently wiping across the surface using the back of your fingers. If cool to the touch, or gripped by the surface, it is still wet underneath.

**1.** When fully dry, the mask can be partially [**A**] or fully removed [**B**] with your fingers.

**2.** A kneadable putty rubber [**C**] will do the job more efficiently, but with less sensitivity. As you go, stroke the surface gently with the fingertips to identify the hidden areas of mask.

**3.** Never pull the mask from the surface [**D**] as this can damage the paper.

MASKING FLUID IN PLACE

MASKING FLUID REMOVED

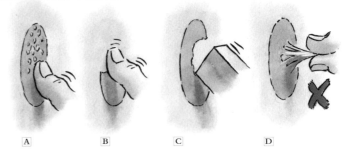

A        B        C        D

◁ **Scuffs angled down the roof** are made with a small round brush, which has been flattened whilst loading the brush across the palette surface. The face of the shoulder is then used to cover the larger areas, previously masked, with light orange. The same brush is reloaded with a darker orange. Still flat, the edge of the flattened shoulder now provides the darker line that suggests the valleys in the rusted tin roof.

◁ **Once the second mask** of the wire fence and the white flowers has been lifted, you can see the effect the contrast makes. With all of the other whites overpainted, the wire and the white flower heads stand out. Suddenly, white becomes a colour, which shows that masking out is a form of painting, in spite of the fact that it is the paper surface which provides the colour.

◁ **It is impossible to paint** the detail of each seed head. Instead, dabbing, scuffing and scumbling is used to exploit the irregular texture of the NOT paper surface. With these techniques the pattern, structure and rhythm of the flower mass can be suggested. This mosaic of strokes can also suggest the movement of its surface as the wind plays gently through the flower heads.

## STAGE 3

Before painting begins, mask the flowers in the foreground and the fence wire. These are the only areas to remain white throughout and need protecting.

A pool of blue grey is drawn across the sky. This will be the smoothest area of the finished painting – a strong contrast for all the textures below, which begin immediately at the buildings.

The rooves are scuffed with colour over previously masked areas. Then, with the same flattened round brush, now used side on, lines are drawn down or across them, while still wet. Yellow-orange scuffs applied across the white walls suggest sunlight.

Whites over the yellow field are given a dry dabbing of yellow-green [Yg] using the brush shoulder.

The cooler shadows ([Yg]plus[bg+ro]), which give structure and depth to the field, are both scuffed and dabbed. Feel for the irregularity of the paper surface as you do this, trying to establish an uneven, natural texture. Look for rhythms and pattern, rather than detail. The stroke of the scuffs is generally downward, but note the lean of these, which helps to provide movement throughout the field. As the strokes are broken by the paper surface, they excite the textures already present.

The yellow blossom and green grasses of the foreground are now all overpainted with small round brushes and Rigger respectively. In the lower shadows, the colours move right through to crimson and purple, which really give a kick to the greens around them. The Rigger strokes of the grass are fluid, being pulled upward, starting thick at the base, becoming fine toward their tips.

# Common problems

**PROBLEM**

*Applying masking fluid too heavily can result in solid, clumsy marks - Fig. 1. As a consequence, many painters are put off using the medium.*

*What a pity to miss the benefits of using such a beneficial medium, for a good controlled mask is perfectly capable of yielding fine highlights and shimmering textures.*

**CAUSE** - The possible causes of this problem include the fact that masking fluid is difficult to see, being close in colour and tone to the paper on which it is being applied.

**SOLUTION** - To get over this, tint it slightly, by adding two or three drops of Indian ink to the bottle containing the masking fluid and shaking vigorously.

**CAUSE** - Some also experience difficulty in loading the masking fluid onto a brush. If the head is overloaded, it will dump a blob of mask onto the surface, as soon as the brush head touches it. Not only will this be ugly, but a pool of masking fluid takes a long time to dry. If it is then accidentally painted over too soon, it may mix with the wet paint and will coagulate as a result.

**SOLUTION** - Tip the palette containing the mask, so that the fluid runs into a corner - Fig. 2. Carefully introduce the brush from the side and once loaded, pull it across the gently curved surface. Excess fluid will be lost at this point and any remaining excess can be brushed out at the palette edge. Not only is the brush correctly loaded now, but it will also be partly flattened by its journey across the palette.

By keeping the angle of the brush low as the mask is applied - Fig. 3, it will skate across the surface of the texture of the paper, leaving the mask only on the prominences. This is all that is required to create successful scuffing and scumbling - Fig. 4.

By applying the mask thinly it dries very swiftly and colour can be applied very soon afterward. However, it is important to ensure the mask is completely dry, always check the surface by touch to determine whether or not it is.

**IMPORTANT**

1. Never apply masking fluid to damp or wet paper, as it can be absorbed by the size and/or fibres and become difficult to remove.

2. Never leave masking fluid on the paper for a long period, as it will deteriorate and become impossible to lift off.

3. If you have to leave the mask on for a couple of days, cover the painting to reduce air contact.

4. Do not use masking fluid that has become thick with age.

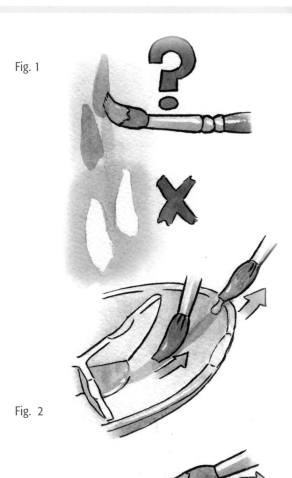

Fig. 1

Fig. 2

Fig. 3

Fig. 4

# Useful information

## PAINTING KIT NEEDED TO COMPLETE THE TUTORIALS IN THIS BOOK

*Watercolour Tube Paints* (pages 14 & 15)
Red-orange (Cadmium Red Deep)
Red-purple (Alizarin Crimson)
Yellow-green (Lemon or Primary Yellow)
Yellow-orange (Cadmium Yellow Deep)
Blue-green (Prussian Blue)
Blue-purple (Ultramarine)

*Watercolour Brushes* (pages 22 & 23)
1 x Small Round (e.g. Size 6)
1 x Large Round (e.g. Size 10)
1 x Rigger (e.g. Size 3)
1 x 44/50mm Hake (around 2")

*Watercolour Palettes* (pages 30 & 31)
Plastic (*Wet on Wet rectangular - with round wells for storing paint in and a large flat area for mixing colours on*)
Ceramic saucer

*Watercolour Paper* (pages 38 & 39)
*Kneadable Putty Rubber*
*Masking Fluid* (small jar)
*0.5mm Automatic Pencil*
*Drawing Board* (to make your own see page 41)
*Gumstrip 50mm* (2")   (see page 41)

## OCCASIONAL GLOSSARY

### TECHNIQUES
**Wet on Dry**
Watercolour paint is applied to a dry surface and brushmarks dry with a hard, clean edge, even when applied lightly.

**Wet on Wet**
Watercolour paint is applied to a wetted surface and brushmarks are soft-edged, even when applied strongly.

**wet-in-wet**
Use of the Wet on Wet technique in restricted areas - also known as restricted wet-into-wet. A small area of painting is wetted with water or colour wash, then painted into while still wet.

**Glaze of colour**
A thin transparent layer of colour wash applied over an already dry painted area.

## REFERENCES
*Colour Reference*
Red-purple [Rp]
Red-orange [Ro]
Blue-purple [Bp]
Blue-green [Bg]
Yellow-orange [Yo]
Yellow-green [Yg]

## COLOUR MIXING
Where the pre-fix letter is shown in capitals this denotes a larger quantity of that particular colour. Conversely, where the pre-fix letter is shown in a lower case, this denotes a smaller quantity of that particular colour.

*E.G.*
**Bp** = *large* amount of blue-purple
**bp** = *small* amount of blue-purple

**Hue, Value, Tone**
*Hue* is a bright primary or secondary colour on the basic colour circle.

*Value* is the degree of lightness or darkness of a colour.

*Tone* is the degree of lightness or darkness of a neutral grey.

*Lights*
The lightest hue of colour in any particular section of a painted area.

*Highlights*
The tiny point of light on the surface at which the light source is reflected. This reflected light maybe white, or a colour.

*Accents*
The darkest points of shadow of an object.

## MATERIALS

*Automatic 0.5 pencil*
A metal or plastic pencil holder in which the thinnest of leads snaps if too much pressure is applied when drawing. Ideal for sketching in the initial composition when working in watercolours, as the linework will not show through the paint.

## ART WORKSHOP WITH PAUL
**Tuition and Guidance for the Artist in Everyone** ♦

*Log on to the artworkshopwithpaul.com website* for downloadable tutorials and Art Clinic, relating to working with watercolours, oils, acrylics, pastels, drawing and other media.

**Check out Paul's Bookshelf** for details of all his books. Visit **Paul's Gallery** and the various galleries showing original paintings, limited edition prints, commissioned work, examples of collected works and work in progress.

**Catch up on the latest news** and details of Art Workshop With Paul Taggart Painting Breaks & Courses.

*Alternatively you can write to*
Art Workshop With Paul Taggart / FS
c/o Promark, Studio 282, 24 Station Square, Inverness, Scotland, IV1 1LD

*Or email*
mail@artworkshopwithpaul.com

## Artstrips©
Fully narrated and detailed step-by-step demonstrations form the basis of all Paul Taggart's live tutorials.

To translate these into publishable form was his ambition and thus it was that twenty years ago he conceived of the Artstrips©.

Unique to Paul Taggart, these Artstrips© are intended as a universally understood method of visually conveying detailed instructions.

# Paul Taggart

*Fine Artist & Author Paul Taggart*

*From his home in the Northern Highlands of Scotland*, professional Fine Artist & Author Paul Taggart shares his enthusiasm for painting with a global audience, through the many books he has written and his extensive website. Paul Taggart's passion for art started at a very early age and ever since gaining a degree in Fine Art over thirty years ago has enjoyed the patronage of collectors, who have purchased an extensive collection of original paintings and limited edition prints.

In line with his belief that everyone should be encouraged to express themselves creatively, Paul Taggart considers it a privilege to have been able to work with aspiring artists throughout that period and to continue to do so. His aim is to provide the right sort of practical help and encouragement in a 'no-nonsense' style that makes the pursuit of painting and drawing accessible to all.

His extensive knowledge across all media in these fields proves invaluable to those following his tutorials, whether through books, the website or when attending his painting breaks and workshops.

Watercolours, oils, acrylics, pastels, drawing and mixed media – all can be developed through Paul Taggart's thorough method of tutoring, honed over many decades of listening to aspiring artists and understanding what they need to achieve their pursuit.

**Art Workshop With Paul Taggart** is the banner under which Paul Taggart offers a variety of learning aids, projects and events, which include books, videos, internet tutorials, painting breaks and courses.

## ACKNOWLEDGEMENTS

*Key people have played a major role in my life and in whom I place my unreserved trust - to them, as always, I say a heartfelt thank you. Eileen (my Life & Business Partner) and I, are delighted to dedicate this series of books to someone who has brought them to life, who wholeheartedly joined us in our work some while ago and now gets to see the fruits of her labours – Sunita Gahir. Since setting the design style for my previous series of six books, she has become an invaluable friend, both privately and professionally.*

*My professional life is split into painting a body of collectable originals, fulfilling commissions, producing material for books and my website, as well as tutoring aspiring painters in painting breaks etc. It is only through the continued patronage of collectors and demand for tutoring from painters that my life as a Professional Fine Artist can continue. Not forgetting those publishers with whom I share a mutual professional trust – most particularly Robert and Susan Guy of Sandcastle Books, who got this series off to a flying start.*

*Paul Taggart*